How Politics Makes Us Sick

How Politics Makes Us Sick

Neoliberal Epidemics

Ted Schrecker and Clare Bambra
Durham University, UK

First published 2015 by
PALGRAVE MACMILLAN

Palgrave Macmillan in the UK is an imprint of Macmillan Publishers Limited, registered in England, company number 785998, of Houndmills, Basingstoke, Hampshire RG21 6XS.

Palgrave Macmillan in the US is a division of St Martin's Press LLC, 175 Fifth Avenue, New York, NY 10010.

Palgrave Macmillan is the global academic imprint of the above companies and has companies and representatives throughout the world.

Palgrave® and Macmillan® are registered trademarks in the United States, the United Kingdom, Europe and other countries.

ISBN 978–1–137–46306–7 hardback
ISBN 978–1–137–46309–8 paperback

This book is printed on paper suitable for recycling and made from fully managed and sustained forest sources. Logging, pulping and manufacturing processes are expected to conform to the environmental regulations of the country of origin.

A catalogue record for this book is available from the British Library.

Library of Congress Cataloging-in-Publication Data
Schrecker, Ted.
How politics makes us sick: neoliberal epidemics / Ted Schrecker and Clare Bambra.
    pages cm
ISBN 978–1–137–46306–7 (hardback) —
ISBN 978–1–137–46309–8 (paperback)
1. Political sociology. 2. Neoliberalism—Social aspects.
3. International economic relations—Social aspects. 4. Welfare state.
I. Bambra, C. (Clare) II. Title.
JA76.S357 2015
306.20973—dc23   2015002382

Contents

Figures, Tables and Boxes

Figures

Tables

Boxes

Preface

Since the early 1980s, neoliberalism has dominated discussions about politics and economics across the globe. The policies of neoliberalism – which place markets at the centre of all economic and social life – have been implemented across many countries and have usually been presented as the only alternative. In this book, we consider the effects of over three decades of these policies with particular reference to the US and the UK. We focus on four areas: obesity, stress, austerity and inequality. We argue that they represent four 'neoliberal epidemics': *neoliberal* because, as we will show, they are associated with or exacerbated by the rise of neoliberal politics; *epidemics* because they are on such an international scale and have been transmitted so quickly across populations that if they were a biological contagion they would be seen as being of epidemic proportions. We also use *epidemic* because our focus is largely on the health effects of these phenomena, now and in the future. We will show that, during the neoliberal era, obesity has emerged as a new and immensely damaging threat to public health across the world; that insecurity likewise is a common condition for vast swathes of the population, with many negative impacts on health; that austerity – a neoliberal response to the 2008 financial crisis – has caused increases in mortality and morbidity; and that economic, social and health inequalities – once in decline across rich industrialized countries – have increased rapidly as a result of the unhindered neoliberal pursuit of profit. All of these epidemics are associated with neoliberalism, and we argue that alternative political and economic choices would have prevented them – or at least reduced their scale – resulting in a healthier 21st century. Neoliberal politics has made us sick.

In Chapter 1, we examine how health varies internationally among rich countries and the social, economic and political reasons for these differences. We also introduce the concept of welfare state regimes. We then outline the rise of neoliberal economics and politics, particularly in the US and the UK, defining their key aspects and drawing parallels with earlier forms of liberal economics in the 19th century.

In Chapter 2, we start with an overview of our first neoliberal epidemic – obesity. Over the last 30 years, obesity rates have doubled in countries such as the UK and the US, with over 20 and 30 per cent (respectively) of adults now considered obese – an epidemic which has been transmitted to our children, as well. We outline the contours of the epidemic, the serious health effects of obesity and the influence of neoliberal economic policies in shaping the development and spread of the disease, and use international comparisons to show how things are – or could be – different in countries that have made different political choices.

Chapter 3 focuses on the neoliberal epidemic of insecurity. Here we argue that neoliberalism has made the labour market and the world of work far less secure and, consequently, more stressful and health damaging. This insecurity manifests itself through reductions in workplace rights, job security, pay levels and welfare rights (so-called flexibility). We argue that this has led to large increases in chronic stress across the populations of many countries (and particularly in the most vulnerable groups), resulting in a myriad of chronic diseases, including musculoskeletal pain and cardiovascular disease. International comparisons are made with countries that have taken a less neoliberal political path.

Chapter 4 examines austerity as a neoliberal epidemic, a particular political and ideological response to the financial crisis of 2008. We describe the politics of this and draw historical comparisons with earlier periods of cuts in social protection. We outline the economic, social and health effects, with a particular focus on the US and the UK, contrasting the experiences in these – two of the most neoliberal countries in the world – with other international experiences where countries have responded to the crisis with state spending rather than public sector cuts.

Chapter 5 examines how neoliberalism has led to an increase in inequalities – economic inequalities, social inequalities and, particularly, health inequalities. We explore trends in inequality at macro, national levels and also draw on three case studies that show different facets of inequality in the UK and the US today: how neoliberalism has exacerbated spatial inequalities in health within England; how neoliberalism has fuelled incarceration rates in the US; and how neoliberal approaches to public services have been played out through the privatization of the English National Health Service (NHS). We also draw on research showing the importance of equality for public health.

In Chapter 6, we outline some common themes shared across the four neoliberal epidemics that we have identified: some reflections of the evidence of the ill-health effects of neoliberalism and the likely inter-generational transmission of its epidemics. We conclude the book by outlining alternative views of the future of health – both pessimistic and optimistic – arguing that the epidemics of neoliberalism require a political cure.

Acknowledgements

Ted Schrecker received no specific funding for the preparation of this manuscript, but would like to thank Durham University for the extraordinary environment that made its completion possible. Clare Bambra is funded by a Leverhulme Trust Research Leadership Award (reference RL-2012-006) to investigate austerity and health inequalities.

Figure 2.4 is reproduced under an Unrestricted Creative Commons Licence.

Figure 3.4 is reproduced with permission from the publisher John Wiley & Sons.

Figures 4.1, 4.2, 5.2, 5.3 and 5.4 are reproduced with the permission of the Centre for Local Economic Strategies. We would like to thank Ben Barr (University of Liverpool) for supplying the artwork.

Figure 5.1 is reproduced under the Open Government Licence with the permission of the Marmot Review.

We would like to thank Kate Pickett for supplying artwork for Figures 5.5, 5.6 and 5.7, and both her and her co-author Richard Wilkinson for allowing free reproduction of this important material.

1
Introduction: Politics and Health

In this introductory chapter we examine how health varies internationally among rich countries and the social, economic and political reasons for these differences. We also introduce the concept of welfare state regimes. We then outline the rise of neoliberal economics and politics, particularly in the US and the UK, defining their key aspects, and draw parallels with earlier forms of liberal economics in the 19th century.

On the health of nations

It is well known that the health of populations varies internationally. Most notably, there are considerable differences in life expectancy (how long someone is expected to live on average) and infant mortality rates (IMR; deaths of children aged under one year old), particularly between Western countries and Africa and Asia. United Nations data show that average life expectancy for men and women in countries like Sierra Leone or Nigeria is as low as 50 years, while in countries like the UK, America, France or Sweden it is over 75 years. These differences are due to economic development: countries in Western Europe, Australasia and North America enjoy the health benefits associated with much higher gross domestic product (GDP) per capita, such as adequate nutrition, access to at least basic medical care, safe drinking water and sanitation, and (for the most part) access to adequate incomes for sustaining the minimum daily activities required for healthy living. The considerable differences that exist *between* Western countries are much less often remarked upon.

Table 1.1 ranks life expectancy at birth among 19 high-income countries for the five decades between 1960 and 2010. This shows that there are considerable differences between the top-performing countries in

Table 1.1 International rankings for life expectancy (*n* years at birth for men and women), 1960–2010

Rank	1960		1970		1980		1990		2000		2010	
1	Norway	73.8	Sweden	74.7	Iceland	76.7	Japan	78.9	Japan	81.2	Japan	83
2	Netherlands	73.5	Iceland	74.3	Japan	76.1	Iceland	78	Iceland	80.1	Switzerland	82.6
3	Sweden	73	Norway	74.3	Norway	75.9	Canada	77.6	Switzerland	79.9	Italy	82
4	Iceland	72.8	Netherlands	73.7	Netherlands	75.8	Sweden	77.6	Italy	79.8	Australia	81.8
5	Denmark	72.4	Denmark	73.3	Sweden	75.8	Switzerland	77.5	Sweden	79.7	Iceland	81.5
6	Switzerland	71.4	Switzerland	73.1	Switzerland	75.6	Italy	77.1	Australia	79.3	Sweden	81.5
7	Canada	71.3	Canada	72.8	Canada	75.3	Australia	77	Canada	79	France	81.3
8	New Zealand	71.1	France	72.2	Australia	74.5	Netherlands	77	France	79	Norway	81.2
9	Australia	70.9	Italy	72	Denmark	74.3	France	76.8	Norway	78.8	Ireland	81
10	UK	70.8	Japan	72	France	74.3	Norway	76.7	New Zealand	78.3	New Zealand	81
11	France	70.3	UK	71.8	Italy	74	Belgium	76.1	Austria	78.2	Canada	80.8
12	Ireland	70	New Zealand	71.5	USA	73.7	UK	75.7	Germany	78.2	Netherlands	80.8
13	Belgium	69.8	Ireland	71.2	Finland	73.6	Austria	75.6	Netherlands	78	Austria	80.7
14	Italy	69.8	Belgium	71	Belgium	73.3	New Zealand	75.5	UK	77.9	UK	80.6
15	USA	69.8	USA	70.9	New Zealand	73.2	Germany	75.3	Belgium	77.8	Germany	80.5
16	Germany	69.1	Australia	70.8	UK	73.2	USA	75.3	Finland	77.7	Belgium	80.3
17	Finland	69	Finland	70.8	Germany	72.9	Finland	75	Denmark	76.8	Finland	80.2
18	Austria	68.7	Germany	70.5	Ireland	72.8	Denmark	74.9	USA	76.7	Denmark	79.3
19	Japan	67.8	Austria	70	Austria	72.6	Ireland	74.9	Ireland	76.6	USA	78.7
Average		70.8		72.2		74.4		76.4		78.6		81.0

Notes:
1. Canada: 1960 uses 1961 data, 1970 uses 1971 data and 2010 uses 2008 data.
2. New Zealand: 1960 uses 1961 data.
3. Italy: 1960 uses 1961 data, 1970 uses 1971 data and 2010 uses 2009 data.
Source: OECD (2013).

each decade and the worst-performing countries. All of these countries are high-income countries, and, indeed, the US has the largest and best-performing economy throughout the 50-year period. However, the US is consistently one of the worst-performing countries in terms of life expectancy – in 1960 and 1970 it is ranked 15th, in 1980 it is 12th, but then falls in 1990 to 16th, in 2000 to 18th and in 2010 it is at the bottom: 19th of 19, with a life expectancy of more than two years less than the average and over four years less than Japan, the best-performing country. Table 1.2 shows an even starker pattern for IMR (deaths per 1000 live births), with the US falling from being a mid-table performer in 1960 (11th) to being the worst-performing country since 1990. The US is consistently towards the bottom of the health rankings among the richest nations. This phenomenon is known as the US health disadvantage, and is of such concern that it was subject to a special investigation, the results of which were published by the US National Academies of Science in 2013 (see Woolf and Aron, 2013).[1]

What explains these differences? One conventional explanation has to do with national variations in health behaviours (i.e. between-country differences in diet, smoking, exercise and alcohol consumption, for example, which can lead to differences in the prevalence of such conditions as cardiovascular disease) or in access to and quality of health care services in each country (Woolf and Aron, 2013). However, these explanations have been found to be wanting, especially in regard to the US health disadvantage (Beckfield and Bambra, 2012). Even where they provide a partial answer, they also raise a question: *why* would behaviours differ in this way? Other explanations are therefore required, and the data in Tables 1.1 and 1.2 may hold the explanatory key as, alongside a US health *disadvantage*, there is also evidence of a health *advantage* for other countries – particularly Sweden, Norway and Japan – which are frequently ranked across the decades in the top ten countries in terms of life expectancy and IMR. Why do these countries do so much better than the US?

Social determinants of health

To answer this question, we begin with the story of one country. In the 1970s, researchers and policy-makers in the UK confronted a puzzle. Despite a generation of access to health care that was free at the point of use for the entire population under the National Health Service (NHS) established in 1948, health inequalities between rich and poor remained stubbornly persistent. The report that was commissioned as a way of

Table 1.2 International rankings for infant mortality (deaths per 1000 live births), 1960–2010

Rank	1960		1970		1980		1990		2000		2010	
1	Iceland	13.0	Sweden	11.0	Sweden	6.9	Japan	4.6	Iceland	3.0	Iceland	2.2
2	Norway	16.0	Norway	11.3	Japan	7.5	Finland	5.6	Japan	3.2	Japan	2.3
3	Netherlands	16.5	Netherlands	12.7	Finland	7.6	Iceland	5.9	Sweden	3.4	Finland	2.3
4	Sweden	16.6	Japan	13.1	Iceland	7.7	Sweden	6.0	Norway	3.8	Sweden	2.5
5	Australia	20.2	Iceland	13.2	Norway	8.1	Switzerland	6.8	Finland	3.8	Norway	2.8
6	Finland	21.0	Finland	13.2	Denmark	8.4	Canada	6.8	Italy	4.3	Italy	3.4
7	Switzerland	21.1	Denmark	14.2	Netherlands	8.6	Norway	6.9	Germany	4.4	Germany	3.4
8	Denmark	21.5	Switzerland	15.1	Switzerland	9.1	Germany	7.0	France	4.5	Denmark	3.4
9	UK	22.5	New Zealand	16.7	France	10.0	Netherlands	7.1	Belgium	4.8	Belgium	3.5
10	New Zealand	22.6	Australia	17.9	Canada	10.4	France	7.3	Austria	4.8	France	3.6
11	USA	26.0	France	18.2	Australia	10.7	Denmark	7.5	Switzerland	4.9	Switzerland	3.8
12	Canada	27.3	UK	18.5	Ireland	11.1	Austria	7.8	Netherlands	5.1	Netherlands	3.8
13	France	27.7	Canada	18.8	UK	12.1	UK	7.9	Australia	5.2	Ireland	3.8
14	Ireland	29.3	Ireland	19.5	Belgium	12.1	Belgium	8.0	Denmark	5.3	Austria	3.9
15	Japan	30.7	USA	20.0	Germany	12.4	Italy	8.1	Canada	5.3	Australia	4.1
16	Belgium	31.4	Belgium	21.1	USA	12.6	Ireland	8.2	UK	5.6	UK	4.2
17	Germany	35.0	Germany	22.5	New Zealand	13.0	Australia	8.2	Ireland	6.2	Canada	5.1
18	Austria	37.5	Austria	25.9	Austria	14.3	New Zealand	8.4	New Zealand	6.3	New Zealand	5.2
19	Italy	43.9	Italy	29.6	Italy	14.6	USA	9.2	USA	6.9	USA	6.1
Average		25.3		17.5		10.4		7.2		4.8		3.7

Notes:
1. Canada: 2010 uses 2008 data.
2. New Zealand: 2010 uses 2009 data.
Source: OECD (2013).

exploring the puzzle, widely known as the Black Report (reproduced in Townsend et al., 1992), argued that the differences were due to what are now called social determinants of health (following Tarlov, 1996): socioeconomically patterned differences in the conditions under which people are born, grow to adulthood, live, work and grow old. Unfortunately, completion of the Black Report coincided with the election of the Conservative government of Margaret Thatcher, and its policy recommendations and, indeed, conceptual framework were shelved, for official purposes, until a successor report was commissioned by a newly elected Labour government almost 20 years later – the Acheson Report (Bambra et al., 2010b).

To oversimplify a complex history, by the new millennium a growing body of research described how health and illness are influenced by factors other than access to health care and the quality of care: the social determinants of health. In part, this growth of research interest reflected the international influence of the Black Report, but also domestic traditions of health activism outside the high-income world, such as Latin American social medicine. It is fair to say that in the US researchers were slower to take up the challenge of social determinants of health, apart from the specific (and important) issue of racial inequalities. This may be because unequal access to health care in the distinctively market-dominated US health care environment tends to monopolize the policy terrain. Social determinants of health, although not described in those terms, were central to the ambitious policy agenda set out in the 1978 Alma-Ata Declaration calling for 'Health for All in the Year 2000' (World Health Organization, 1978). In 2005, the then-director general of the World Health Organization established a multinational Commission on Social Determinants of Health, headed by noted epidemiologist Sir Michael Marmot – best known at the time for leading the Whitehall studies of British civil servants, which we discuss in later chapters.[2] The Commission's report, published in 2008 (see also the summary that appeared as Marmot et al., 2008), was organized around two central concepts.

The first was socioeconomic gradients in health: nearly ubiquitous inequalities in health outcomes that are related to patterns of social (dis)advantage. Figure 1.1 provides an illustration of such gradients in the proportion of children who die before the age of five (the under-5 mortality rate, or U5MR) in six very different lower- and middle-income countries (LMICs). This figure illustrates what is called an inverse gradient: in other words, the higher the household's income quintile, the lower the U5MR for households in that quintile. The second was health

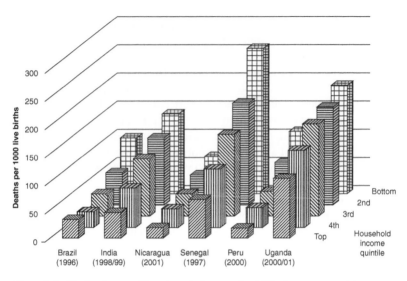

Figure 1.1   Under-5 mortality rates, six low- and middle-income countries
Source: Data from Gwatkin et al. (2007).

equity: the absence of inequalities in health that are unfair or unjust and avoidable. The Commission was clear that it considered *most* such health inequalities, within and among countries, to be avoidable and therefore inequitable (Commission on Social Determinants of Health, 2007, p. 1). Its final report, released in 2008, began with the observation that '[S]ocial injustice is killing people on a grand scale' and continued:

> The poor health of the poor, the social gradient in health within countries, and the marked health inequities between countries are caused by the unequal distribution of power, income, goods, and services, globally and nationally, the consequent unfairness in the immediate, visible circumstances of people's lives – their access to health care, schools, and education, their conditions of work and leisure, their homes, communities, towns, or cities – and their chances of leading a flourishing life. This unequal distribution of health-damaging experiences is in no sense a 'natural' phenomenon but is the result of a toxic combination of poor social policies and programs, unfair economic arrangements, and bad politics.
>
> (Commission on Social Determinants of Health, 2008, p. 1)

The Commission's perspective is noteworthy for at least three reasons. First, this is not the kind of language one usually encounters in United

Nations system documents. Second, it suggests that inequalities in health *within* and *among* countries may be explicable with reference to the same body, or at least overlapping bodies, of research evidence. Third, it emphasizes the importance of factors other than health care, and – in policy terms – involving both agencies of government and private sector actors outside the health care system or industry.

Canadian researchers Evans and Stoddart (1990), two of the conceptual pioneers in thinking about these questions, described an approach to health that they called the thermostat model, using an analogy to home heating. At least before the energy crises of the 1970s, we tended to respond to chilly rooms by turning up the thermostat. Similarly, health policy often still tends to respond to increases in illness by turning up the health care thermostat: spending more on health care. One of their arguments was that this could quickly become unaffordable; Evans, at least, was later to qualify this by noting that definitions of affordability are contested political terrain. Another argument, more directly relevant to our project, was that it might be more effective to reduce illness by the policy analogues of insulating walls and double-glazing windows. Policies to reduce illness, improve health and reduce or eliminate socioeconomic gradients in health by way of acting on social determinants of health are usefully thought of in this way. There is nothing new about these recognitions. Rather, they represent a rediscovery of earlier insights, going back to the 19th century, about the relation between the conditions of life and (ill) health. We explore this point in the last section of the chapter.

The political economy of health

Unfortunately, a list of social determinants of health that is recognized as authoritative does not exist in the same way as (for example) a list of the risk factors for cardiovascular disease. This is partly a function of past allocations of resources for health research, which have overwhelmingly favoured curative, medical approaches (Östlin et al., 2011), in recent years especially those with potential for commercial application – arguably yet another neoliberal epidemic, but one unfortunately outside the scope of this book. Here, we refer frequently to various bodies of research evidence on social determinants of health, but also ask a further set of questions. What affects the social determinants of health? Why are there such considerable variations among and within countries in the distribution of opportunities to lead a healthy life? Epidemiologist Geoffrey Rose described this as investigating 'the causes of the causes', a phrase later often used by Marmot.

A shorthand description of our approach to answering those questions involves the political economy of health. Historian Anne-Emanuelle Birn and colleagues (2009, pp. 132–148) distinguish among biomedical, behavioural and political economy approaches to health. The biomedical model focuses on possibilities for cure and views differences in health as differences among individuals; the behavioural approach focuses on what are widely referred to as lifestyle choices (smoking, alcohol consumption, healthy diets, seatbelt use) while normally neglecting the larger contextual influences (low incomes that make healthy diets unaffordable, intensive marketing of energy-dense convenience foods to children – examined in more detail in Chapter 2). The political economy approach, by contrast, focuses on 'social, political and economic structures and relations' that may be, and often are, outside the control of the individuals they affect: health is politically determined (Bambra et al., 2005). As epidemiologist Nancy Krieger describes the core of the political economy approach, patterns of health and disease are '*produced*, literally and metaphorically, by the structures, values and priorities of political and economic systems ... Health inequities are thus posited to arise from whatever is each society's form of social inequality, defined in relation to power, property and privilege' (Krieger, 2013). Another way of expressing this idea comes from work by Diderichsen and colleagues, who argued for explaining socially patterned disparities in health in terms of how social stratification (the unequal distribution of resources and opportunities) generates differences in exposures to risks of illness, vulnerabilities to those exposures and consequences of ill health. Further, they argued that explanations must venture upstream from the observed facts of stratification to consider 'those central engines in society that generate and distribute power, wealth and risks' (Diderichsen et al., 2001, p. 16). In 2014, the *Lancet*–University of Oslo Commission on Global Governance for Health took a further step by putting forward the concept of political determinants of health, insisting that '[c]onstruing socially and politically created health inequities as problems of technocratic or medical management depoliticises social and political ills' (Ottersen et al., 2014, p. 636).

We argue that one of the main reasons health varies so considerably between economically developed countries is the differences in the political economy of such countries (Bambra, 2011; Beckfield and Bambra, 2012) – differences in how those central engines operate, who operates them and with what priorities. While all these countries are in economic terms capitalist, in that their economic activity is organized primarily through the operation of markets, and in political terms liberal democracies, they nevertheless differ in important ways in terms of how they implement, manage and structure their societies. This leads to important differences in the social determinants of health, both among and within those countries. These differences are usefully captured through the concept of *welfare state regimes* (Esping-Andersen, 1990). The welfare state is a contested term within social and political analysis (Eikemo and Bambra, 2008). Conventionally, the term has been used to describe state provision of education, health care, housing and social protection (cash benefits for the unemployed, the sick or the old, for example) and other social services (Bambra, 2011, p. 24). More broadly, the welfare state can be considered as a particular form of capitalist state or a specific type of society, which emerged in advanced market democracies in Western countries during the early post-World War II period (Esping-Andersen, 1990). For most of the 19th century, there was minimal state provision of welfare beyond very basic 'poor relief' – the provision of basic food rations and shelter (often provided via institutions such as the English workhouse system). Beyond these provisions, welfare came via family members or charity (particularly the church). This began to change in the early 20th century with the introduction of rudimentary and highly selective state-organized welfare systems which provided basic pensions, unemployment and sickness benefits funded via social insurance payments (e.g. the 1911 National Insurance Act in the UK, or the welfare innovations put in place in the 1880s by Otto von Bismarck in Germany). At the time, non-workers – a category that included most women – were typically excluded from such schemes.

Only after World War II was what is often referred to as the Keynesian welfare state established. To a greater or lesser extent, this 'golden age' of welfare state capitalism was characterized by centralism, universalism and Keynesian economics (active macroeconomic management by the state such as interventionist fiscal policy, a large public sector and a mixed economy), full (male) employment and high public expenditure, and the promotion of mass consumption via a redistributive tax and welfare system. There was also a mainstream political consensus in favour of the welfare state and the redistribution it effected. During this age of welfare state expansion (1940s–1960s), Western countries experienced significant improvements to public housing, health care and the other main social determinants of health. However, golden age welfare states varied considerably in the services they provided and the generosity and coverage of social protection.

Welfare states can be divided into three different types or regimes (Esping-Andersen, 1990): liberal (sometimes referred to as Anglo-Saxon),

Table 1.3   Welfare state regimes

Liberal	Bismarckian	Social democratic
Australia	Austria	Denmark
Canada	Belgium	Finland
Ireland	France	Iceland
New Zealand	Germany	Sweden
UK	Italy	Norway
US	Japan	
	Switzerland	
	Netherlands	

Bismarckian and social democratic (or Scandinavian) (Table 1.3). These are described below, although there were and are significant differences even within these regimes: for example, New Zealand and the UK provided national public health services, while the US relied (and still relies) in the first instance on private insurance, albeit with expanding publicly financed provision for the old (Medicare) and the extremely poor (Medicaid). There are also debates among academics about the number of different regimes and about which countries should be in which group (for further discussion see Bambra, 2007), with some researchers, for example, adding a distinctive Southern welfare state regime describing Greece, Spain and Portugal.

Broadly speaking, in the welfare states of the liberal regime (Australia, Canada, Ireland, New Zealand, the UK and the US), state provision of welfare was and is fairly minimal; social insurance benefits were modest and often contingent on meeting strict entitlement criteria; recipients were often subject to means testing; and receipt was stigmatized. In this model, even in the post-war period, the dominance of the market was encouraged by guaranteeing only a minimum level of support and by subsidizing private welfare schemes. In the liberal welfare state regime a stark division existed between those, largely the poor, who relied on state aid and those who were able to afford private provision. The Bismarckian welfare state regime (Austria, Belgium, France, Germany, Italy, Japan, Switzerland and the Netherlands) was characterized by its 'status differentiating' welfare programs, in which benefits were often directly related to earnings or contributions, administered through employers or employer organizations and geared towards maintaining existing social hierarchies. The role of the family was also emphasized and the redistributive impact of this regime was minimized. However, the market was more marginalized than in the liberal regime.

The social democratic regime type (Denmark, Finland, Iceland, Sweden and Norway) was characterized by universalism; comparatively generous social transfers; a commitment to full employment and income protection; and a strongly interventionist state in terms of both the economy and regulation (e.g. a strong public health policy). The state was actively used to promote social equality through a redistributive social security system. Unlike the other welfare state regimes, the social democratic regime type promoted an equality of the highest standards, not an equality of minimal needs. It should be noted that the Finnish welfare state was not developed until the 1960s, which may explain its poorer showing in Tables 1.1 and 1.2. The welfare state is thereby understood as more than a set of transfers and services. It consists of systems and processes that themselves shape society and influence stratification (Bambra, 2011, p. 26), and is, therefore, potentially an important macro-level political and economic determinant of health.

Comparative research on the social determinants of health has increasingly concluded that population health is enhanced by the relatively generous and universal welfare provision of the social democratic countries, especially in contrast to the liberal welfare states (Bambra, 2012). In terms of mortality, studies have consistently shown that IMRs vary significantly by welfare regime type, with rates lowest in the Nordic countries and highest in the liberal countries. For example, Navarro and colleagues (2003, 2006) found that those countries which have had long periods of government by redistributive political parties (most notably the social democratic countries) have experienced lower IMR and, to a lesser extent, increased life expectancy at birth. Mackenbach and McKee (2013) also found that social democratic rule was beneficial for health, particularly in terms of preventive health policy (most notably in terms of alcohol and tobacco control policy). These findings were reinforced by Chung and Muntaner's (2007) analysis of welfare state regimes, in which they found that around 20 per cent of the difference in IMR between rich countries, and 10 per cent of the difference in low birth weight babies (LBW), could be explained by the type of welfare state. The social democratic countries had significantly lower IMR and LBW than the other welfare state regimes. An innovative study by Lundberg and colleagues (2008) examined the influence of two key social democratic welfare state policies – support for dual-earners (where both men and women are encouraged to work) and generous basic pensions – on IMR and old age excess mortality in 18 of the richest countries. They found that increases in support for the dual-earner family model decreased IMR. Similarly, increases in the generosity of basic old age pensions led to decreases in old age excess mortality. Coburn (2004) concluded that those countries which were the least neoliberal in their economic and social policy orientation (i.e. the social democratic welfare states) had significantly lower IMR, lower overall mortality rates and less mortality at younger ages. This study also suggested that welfare state regime might be the mediating link between national economic wealth (GDP per capita) and mortality.

Different commentators have chosen to privilege particular explanations for this social democratic supremacy (Bambra, 2012). For example, the key characteristics of the social democratic welfare state package (universalism, generous replacement rates, extensive welfare services) result in narrower income inequalities and higher levels of decommodification (whereby the ability to have a decent standard of living is not dependent on labour market position, i.e. what job or income you have), both of which are associated with better population health (Wilkinson and Pickett, 2010). Coburn (2004), along with Navarro and colleagues (2003, 2006), has also highlighted the importance of the long-term accumulative positive effect on income inequalities of governance by pro-redistribution political parties. Other commentators have also suggested that increased gender equality within the Scandinavian countries may be another incremental factor behind their better health outcomes (Bambra et al., 2009). Better public health regulation in countries with longer periods of social democratic government is also something highlighted by Mackenbach and McKee (2013). Furthermore, proponents of the social capital approach have highlighted the high levels of social cohesion and integration within social democratic societies, something which has also been associated with better population health (Kawachi et al., 1997).

The rise of neoliberalism

What has been called the golden age of the welfare state effectively ended with the economic crisis of the 1970s and the rise of neoliberalism. The term itself is confusing to many North Americans, who associate the word 'liberal' with what passes for the left of the political spectrum in their part of the world. Historical sociologist Margaret Somers (2008) suggests instead the phrase 'market fundamentalism' – ironically borrowed from currency speculator George Soros, one of the world's richest men, who owes his fortune in large measure to the globalization of financial markets that neoliberalism brought about. Although many definitions can be found in the academic literature, the fundamental presuppositions of neoliberalism are as follows. First, markets are the normal, natural and preferable way of organizing most, if not all, forms of human interaction. They can be viewed as preferable either (a) because they maximize freedom of choice; (b) because they lead to 'efficient' outcomes, which maximize welfare, since by definition all market exchanges are voluntary[3]; or, (c) often, both. Second, the primary function of the state is to ensure the efficient functioning of markets. Third, institutions or policies that lead to outcomes different from those that would be expected from a market functioning as markets are supposed to in economics textbooks require justification (for a more detailed inventory, see Ward and England, 2007, pp. 4–6).

Neoliberalism owes much conceptually to the work of Austrian political theorist Friedrich Hayek, and in terms of its institutional provenance to the Mont Pelerin society that he helped to found in 1947. Although popularized by economist Milton Friedman and a variety of well-funded think tanks, the core tenets of neoliberalism remained on the margins of mainstream politics in the high-income world until the 1970s (Marchak, 1991, pp. 93–100; Harvey, 2005, pp. 19–22). At that point the economic uncertainties of 'stagflation' – the simultaneous occurrence of high inflation and high unemployment – created a newly receptive climate among both elites and, in many countries, electorates. Various narratives of the advance of neoliberalism can be found in the literature. One regards neoliberal policies as pragmatic responses to a changing global economic environment that was largely outside the control of individual national governments. Under these new conditions, neoliberal policies were the only ones that 'worked' (see e.g. Fourcade-Gourinchas and Babb, 2002). Another views neoliberalism as a political project aimed at the restoration of class power that had been eroded by the rise of the welfare state and associated redistributive policies, although 'not necessarily...the restoration of economic power to the same people' (Harvey, 2005, p. 31). These narratives are not mutually exclusive. It is clear, however, that neoliberalism is best understood as having multiple dimensions, including concrete policy programs and innovations (e.g. welfare state retrenchment and 'workfare'), more general reorganization of state institutions (e.g. privatization and contracting out), and an ideology (Ward and England, 2007). Perhaps even more importantly, the advance of neoliberalism, or neoliberalization (the process by which societies become more neoliberal), involves not so much an actual shrinking of the state as a reorganization of the state around different functions and priorities: 'the extension of market rule and disciplines, *principally by means of state power*' (Tickell and Peck, 2003,

p. 165, emphasis added). A related distinction is that drawn by Peck and Tickell (2002) between 'roll-back' and 'roll-out' neoliberalism – the idea here being that, while the state is retreating from some activities, such as providing income support or regulating labour markets, it is simultaneously expanding or intensifying its activities in others, such as surveillance of benefit claimants or policing and imprisonment.

Whichever narrative of the political ascendancy of neoliberalism one accepts, the election of the Conservative government of Margaret Thatcher in the UK in 1979 and of Republican US president Ronald Reagan in 1980 represented key turning points, although the subsequent trajectories of neoliberalism in their respective countries were mediated by important differences in their political systems (King and Wood, 1999). Our concern in this book is primarily with domestic consequences, although it is important to recognize the international dimensions as well. The elections of Thatcher and Reagan coincided with the onset of the first international debt crisis, signalled shortly afterward by Mexico's temporary default on loans not only from the World Bank but also from major US banks – a development that raised concern about the stability of financial systems in the industrialized world (see generally Lever and Huhne, 1985). The result was an expansion of structural adjustment lending by the World Bank and International Monetary Fund (IMF), in which policy-making was and is dominated by the US and a few other high-income economies. The conditions attached to these loans emphasized reduction of subsidies for basic items of consumption such as food; rapid removal of barriers to imports and foreign direct investment; reductions in state expenditures, particularly on social programs such as health, education, water/sanitation and housing; and rapid privatization of state-owned enterprises, on the presumption that private service provision was inherently more efficient, and that proceeds from privatization could be used to ensure debt repayment (Milward, 2000; Babb, 2005). In other words, the World Bank and IMF promoted multiple, more or less coordinated domestic policies of neoliberalizing national economies while integrating national economies into the global marketplace. In Chapter 4, we explore a provocative analogy between these policy changes and similar policies adopted within high-income countries. Here, it suffices to note a retrospective observation by a panel of social scientists concerned with prospects for sustainable democracy: 'An alliance of the international financial institutions, the private banks, and the Thatcher [UK]-Reagan [US]-Kohl [West German] governments was willing to use its political and economic power to back its ideological predilections' (Przeworski et al., 1995, p. 5).

Initially in the Anglo-American countries, but then more broadly, the political consensus of the golden age – sometimes described as the post-war settlement between labour and capital – began to break down as governments started to dismantle and restructure the welfare state. The 'reforms' were characterized by the privatization and marketization of welfare services; entitlement restrictions and increased qualifying conditions for benefits, and a shift towards targeting and means testing; cuts or limited increases to the actual cash values of benefits; modified funding arrangements (with a shift away from business taxation); and an increased emphasis on an active rather than a passive welfare system (Bambra et al., 2010a). As Taylor-Gooby (2008, p. 4) has put it, these changes reflect 'a shift towards the view that the role of government is to promote national competitiveness in an increasingly international market, and away from a passive providing state to one which seeks to enhance self-activity, responsibility and mobilization into paid work among citizens' through social investment.

In the rest of the book, we concentrate on the manifestations of neoliberalism and the process of neoliberalization in the UK and the US – two of the countries with which we are most familiar, and in many respects those that have proceeded farthest down the neoliberal road. We supplement this discussion, as appropriate, with comparative data on other high-income countries. To provide a comparative perspective, the progress of neoliberalization is shown for each welfare state regime in Figure 1.2. This uses data from the 'Economic Freedom of the World Index' (Fraser Institute, 2013), produced by Canada's neoliberal Fraser Institute – established in 1972 with funding from many of Canada's largest corporations, many of them subsidiaries of transnationals (Marchak, 1991, p. 112). The index measures size of government (expenditures, taxes, etc.), legal structure and security of property rights, access to finance, freedom to trade internationally and the regulation of credit, labour and business. It produces a scale of 1–10, with higher scores representing higher levels of 'economic freedom' as defined by neoliberals – meaning fewer rights for workers, lower taxes on businesses, easier (although not necessarily less costly) access to credit and less state regulation (i.e. freedom for capital, not necessarily for people). So, Figure 1.2 shows how neoliberal 'economic freedom' has increased since 1980 across *all* of the welfare state regimes. It is much higher in 2010 than in 1980. However, the liberal welfare state regime has consistently higher neoliberalism scores than the other welfare state regimes.

This neoliberal restructuring of the welfare state has been analysed by some commentators as a shift from Keynesian welfare state capitalism, which could afford and required a high level of public welfare

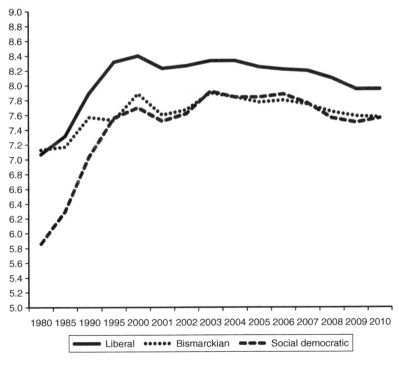

Figure 1.2   The rise of neoliberalism, 1980–2010, by welfare state regime

expenditure, to a system of 'workfare state' capitalism (Bambra, 2009) in which high welfare expenditure is considered to be incompatible with a growing and profitable economy. Workfare state capitalism is characterized by decentralization and welfare pluralism (with a strong role for the private sector), the promotion of labour market flexibility, supply-side economics, the subordination of social policy to the demands of the market and a desire to minimize social expenditure. As with welfare states, there are variants of the workfare model, reflecting the historical constraints presented by the policy hangover of existing welfare state regime structures and politics, variations in public opinion between countries, and differences by regime in policy responses to common challenges (Jessop, 1991). The neoliberal workfare state emphasizes the privatization of state enterprise and welfare services and the deregulation of the private sector (Jessop, 1991, p. 95). The neo-Bismarckian workfare state is characterized by an economic policy increasingly geared to the microeconomic level and a smaller role for the state as key welfare services, such as health or pensions, become increasingly self-regulated and welfare becomes more pluralistic and privatized (Jessop, 1991, p. 97). The neo-social democratic response relies on a state-guided approach to economic reorganization. Flexibility is provided through an active labour market policy, epitomized by Denmark's system of 'flexicurity' (Muffels and Wilthagen, 2013), which emphasizes training, skills and mobility while retaining a relatively generous out-of-work benefit system.

It could be inferred from this description that we accept the inevitability of convergence on an economic and social policy model that incorporates and accepts at least some aspects of neoliberalism. This is not the case; we are simply describing comparative patterns. As we note throughout the rest of the book, but especially in our concluding chapter, neoliberalization in the high-income world has been a matter of political choices – choices that could have been made, and in our view should have been made, differently. Countries that have made such different choices continue to survive, and their people continue to thrive – in fact, to do rather better than those living with or under neoliberalism.

Back to the future?

There are clear parallels between neoliberal policy prescriptions and the unfettered liberal capitalism of the 19th century. As political philosopher Alison Jaggar (2002, p. 425) points out, not much is 'neo' or new about neoliberalism. Rather, it represents a return to 'the non-redistributive laissez faire liberalism of the 17th and 18th centuries, which held that the main function of government was to make the world safe and predictable for the participants in a market economy'. In health terms there are also similarities. So, while population health in the industrial revolution of the 18th and 19th centuries was characterized by epidemics in communicable infectious disease (e.g. the cholera outbreak of the 1830s in the UK or the 1890s typhoid epidemic in the US) and the 21st century is plagued by chronic disease (such as cancers and diabetes), we argue that there are striking similarities in terms of both causation and social distribution between the two periods, with income inequalities, poor working conditions, lack of access to services and unequal power distribution dominating in both periods.

In *To Live and Die in America* (2013), economists Robert Chernomas and Ian Hudson argue that in the 18th and 19th centuries the political and economic structures of laissez-faire liberalism, which favoured capital (e.g. factory or mine owners) at the expense of labour (working people), resulted in wide-scale infectious disease epidemics, primarily because the mass of working people were subjected to such poor conditions that they were in no position to physically resist contagion. So, for example, wage levels in the 18th and 19th centuries for labourers were so low that they were barely (and not always even) at subsistence levels, and certainly nowhere near providing the nutrition required to sustain a fully functioning immune system. Similarly, harsh and dangerous industrial working conditions – such as those experienced by coal miners or cotton mill workers (as vividly portrayed in the literature of the day, such as Zola's *Germinal* of 1895, Dickens' *Hard Times* of 1854 and Gaskell's *North and South* of 1855) – were such that they took a major toll on the body and mind. For example, cotton mill workers in Manchester, England, worked 10–16 hours a day, six days a week, in dangerous conditions, with children widely involved and earning only 10–20 per cent of a man's wage, until legislation such as the 1833 Factory Act. Miners regularly worked similar long hours underground manually digging coal, paid by weight of coal not hours worked, and yet still had insufficient funds to adequately feed and clothe themselves and their families. Industrial 'accidents' were commonplace, with, for example, over 330 miners per 100,000 dying each year on the job in the US in the early 1900s (US Bureau of Labor Statistics, 2013). Housing conditions were equally poor, with much of the population inhabiting unsanitary slums – resulting in the quick spread of disease. For example, in New York's 10th ward, as many as 12 families would live on one floor of a small tenement block (Chernomas and Hudson, 2013). In Liverpool, the medical officer for health, Dr William Duncan, reported that 40,000 of the population lived in damp, unventilated cellars (Chadwick, 1843).

Such were the inequalities in this period that Edwin Chadwick's *Report on the Sanitary Conditions of the Labouring Population of Great Britain* found that the life expectancy of labourers was significantly lower than that of the gentry, and that this varied between rural areas (where agricultural labour dominated) and the industrial cities (where factory work was the norm). His data are presented in Table 1.4 alongside similar data (comparisons are indicative only) from today that compare life expectancy of living in the most and least deprived parts of a city or area. The picture is one of clear inequalities that have remained, despite huge increases in overall life expectancy between the 1840s and today. Further, the inequalities within urban areas between the 'haves' and the 'have-nots' were higher in the 1840s in the urban areas, and this also remains the case today.

Table 1.4 Average life expectancy in years (men) by occupation in England, 1840s and 2010s

	1840s			2010s		
	Gentry and professionals	Labourers	Gap	Living in least deprived areas	Living in most deprived areas	Gap
Rural/Agricultural						
Bath	55	25	30	80	75	5
Kendal	45	34	11	78	70	8
Rutland	52	38	14	82	76	6
Wiltshire	50	33	17	80	73	7
Urban/Industrial						
Bolton	34	18	16	77	63	14
Bethnal Green (London)	45	16	29	77	65	12
Liverpool	35	15	20	75	64	11
Manchester	38	17	21	74	63	11

Source: Adapted from Chadwick (1843) and London Health Observatory (2012).

The popularized view is that the infectious diseases of the 19th century were overcome by science – with medical advances in treatments and vaccinations. However, Chernomas and Hudson persuasively argue that changes in the economic and political determinants of infectious disease were more important than tackling germs. Indeed, much of the decrease in infectious disease in rich industrial countries predated the discovery and mass application of medical interventions (McKeown, 1976). Infectious diseases were, in fact, brought under control when organized resistance by labour, via trade unions, resulted in improvements to wages, working conditions, welfare services and housing (Chernomas and Hudson, 2014). Most notably, the Factory Acts of the 1800s in the UK gradually limited the use of child labour and introduced the eight-hour working day; rising wages enabled access to better nutrition; the welfare state emerged, starting late in the 19th/early 20th century, as noted earlier; and sanitary reforms and slum clearances eliminated the worst health-damaging environmental exposures. These beneficial reforms were strengthened and institutionalized in the postwar period with the advent of the welfare state and a more regulatory and interventionist approach to the economy.

Today, the major killers in rich countries are cancers and heart disease. Obviously, smoking plays a role in both of these diseases. However, there are also other factors – the social and political determinants of health – that contribute. For example, as we show in chapters 2 and 3, obesity (a new form of malnutrition) is related to several aspects of life under neoliberalism, and stress arising from economic insecurity is associated with an increased risk of heart disease. The emergence of such chronic killers pre-dates neoliberalism; cancer and heart disease took over from infectious disease as the major causes of death by the 1940s. However, as with 18th- and 19th-century economic liberalism, many of the changes associated with neoliberalism increase our susceptibility to such diseases. The conditions in which we live, work and play remain vital in determining how long we live. So, as workers' rights and job security are eroded in the name of economic freedom (e.g. the attacks on trade unions of the 1980s), wages fall in value (with one in four children in the UK living in poverty, and a healthy diet less affordable for growing numbers of people), welfare is cut-back and restricted, and work-related insecurity increases, neoliberalism is returning us to an environment in which (chronic) disease can flourish. The stark health inequalities noted by Chadwick in the 19th century remain today, as Table 1.4 shows; we elaborate at the start of Chapter 5.

So, while the diseases of today differ significantly from those of the 19th century and there has been a clear *epidemiological transition* from communicable to chronic disease, the determinants of health remain political and economic. These parallels do not augur well for the future of global health, as, in order to increase profits and the 'economic freedom' of the few, the spread of neoliberalism is eroding the conditions conducive to a healthy life for the many. This is the focus of the rest of the book.

The rest of the book

In each of the next four chapters, we describe what we call a neoliberal epidemic, drawing on evidence related to the social determinants of health and an extensive body of social science research, along with some journalism, on the real-world consequences of neoliberalism. We rely on a standard definition of an epidemic as 'a disease that affects a large number of people, with a recent and substantial increase in the number of cases' with a single, identifiable causal agent (Martin and Martin-Granel, 2006, p. 980). 'Epidemic' is also used colloquially to refer to non-medical events – 'to qualify anything that adversely affects a large number of persons or objects and propagates like a disease' (Martin and Martin-Granel, 2006, p. 980). In this book, we use the term 'epidemic' to refer to obesity, insecurity, austerity and inequality. In our view, the common causal agent for these four epidemics is neoliberal politics.

One of the most conspicuous public health trends of the past few decades has been the rise in overweight and obesity – not only in the high-income world, but also, more recently, in countries outside it. In Chapter 2, we situate this trend as a neoliberal epidemic with reference to such factors as the role of intensive marketing of unhealthy, energy-dense foods and the body of evidence that multiple pathways link obesity and economic insecurity.

Economic insecurity itself is the topic of Chapter 3. We explain the rise of economic insecurity with reference to policy choices that neoliberalized labour markets in the US, the UK and (with wide national variation) globally, and connect their consequences with evidence on how neoliberalism can 'get under your skin' by way of material deprivation, but also by way of the physiological consequences of exposure to chronic stress.

In Chapter 4, we turn our attention to the financial crisis that swept across the world in 2008 and provided the impetus (or, perhaps, the pretext) for austerity and the expenditure cutbacks that are now accepted across most of the political spectrum. We explore the crisis as being itself a manifestation of the neoliberal deregulation of financial markets and capital flows, and critique responses to it in terms of their negative impact on the opportunity for many people to lead healthy lives.

The combined impact of financial crisis and austerity as a policy response seems certain to increase inequality within national borders, and, consequently, inequality of health outcomes. In Chapter 5, after a brief review of the evidence supporting this proposition, we describe three specific case examples – two from the UK, one from the US – and conclude with a summary of a body of evidence suggesting that higher levels of economic inequality in a society, or a social unit as small as a metropolitan area, have an adverse impact on average health outcomes across the entire population.

Chapter 6 offers some reflections on the evidence (and the politics of how evidence is used), and explores two somewhat divergent perspectives on prospects for reducing the destructive impact of neoliberalism on health and society by, in effect, reconstructing the post-war settlement, or at least revitalizing the welfare state that it underpinned.

Chapters 2–5 also suggest a number of secondary or cross-cutting issues and arguments, which we highlight at various points and then revisit in Chapter 6.

The first of these is the *individualization of risk and responsibility*. Legal scholars identify as a key element of neoliberalization 'the process whereby a broad range of social issues is being reconstituted, both with respect to causes and solutions, in highly individualized terms. Health care and poverty are treated as individual shortcomings, products of poor individual choices, to be remedied by emphasizing individual responsibility' (Fudge and Cossman, 2002, pp. 21–22, citations omitted) – again a parallel with earlier forms of economic and political liberalism. Fudge and Cossman were thinking in the first instance of ideology and discourse, but there are concrete material dimensions as well, which we discuss in Chapter 3.

A second area involves *the politics of scientific evidence* and its use in public policy. Especially in epidemiology, it is often argued that there is a lack of evidence for health effects of neoliberalism. If one sets the evidentiary bar high enough, then it is always possible to argue that more research is needed (the tobacco industry did this for decades). Because social determinants of health inequalities tend to operate through multiple and complex, macro-level causal pathways, experimental or quasi-experimental studies are often impossible. Thus, we use evidence from a variety of sources, generated using multiple designs and methodologies (including personal observations), to tell our causal story.

A third issue area is *the intergenerational impact of neoliberal epidemics* – in other words, how their effects span generations. There are several potential pathways, including the effects of entrenched structural economic inequality and the associated lack of social mobility; cultural patterns that reinforce disadvantage; and biological mechanisms. Thus, we are probably witnessing a new dimension of the communicable disease problem, with communication occurring over time as well as space – an argument that we expand upon, drawing on evidence from preceding chapters, in Chapter 6.

2
Obesity: How Politics Makes Us Fat

We start with an overview of our first neoliberal epidemic – obesity. Over the last 30 years, obesity rates have doubled in countries such as the UK and the US, with over 20 and 30 per cent (respectively) of adults now considered as obese. We outline the contours of the epidemic, the serious health effects of obesity and the influence of neoliberal economic policies in shaping the development and spread of the disease, and use international comparisons to show how things are – or could be – different in countries that have made different political choices.

Contours of the obesity epidemic

'Number of people claiming benefits because of obesity doubles'; 'Two-thirds of northerners are now obese'; 'Parents of obese 11-year-old arrested on suspicion of child cruelty'. These are just a few of the almost daily headlines in the British tabloid press about the obesity epidemic. In the US, there is similar news saturation on the topic. News stories such as these sometimes seem a bit breathless when describing what is now recognized as an epidemic of overweight and obesity, but behind the headlines lies what Al Gore would call an inconvenient truth.

A 2010 editorial in the *Journal of the American Medical Association* warned: 'If left unchecked, overweight and obesity have the potential to rival smoking as a public health problem, potentially reversing the net benefit that declining smoking rates have had on the US population over the last 50 years' (Gaziano, 2010, p. 275). Overweight and obesity have been growing rapidly throughout the high-income world, and indeed elsewhere, meaning that overweight and obesity may constitute a truly global neoliberal epidemic. At the end of the 1970s it was

23

estimated that 15 per cent of the adult population (age 20–74) of the US were obese – a figure that had not changed much since the start of the 1960s (Ogden and Carroll, 2010). By 2011–2012, the percentage of obese US adults had more than doubled, to 35 per cent (Ogden et al., 2013). Among adolescents (age 12–17 or 12–19, depending on the survey year) the increase is even more striking – from 5 per cent at the end of the 1970s (Glickman et al., 2012) to 9.1 per cent in 1988–1991 (Frederick et al., 2014) and 20.5 per cent in 2011–2012 (Ogden et al., 2014), although most of the increase appears to have occurred before the new millennium. In the UK, it is estimated that the prevalence of obesity nearly tripled between 1980 and 2002, from 6 per cent among men and 8 per cent among women to 23 per cent of men and 25 per cent of women (Rennie and Jebb, 2005). Among children (age 2–15) in England, the prevalence of obesity is estimated to have increased from 11 per cent among boys and 12 per cent of girls in 1995 to 18–19 per cent for both sexes in 2005, with a slight decline since then (Health and Social Care Information Centre, 2014). Here, as elsewhere, we focus on the US and the UK, but estimates for a much larger number of high-income countries (Figure 2.1) show that the pattern is consistent,[4] albeit with considerable variation among countries of differing welfare state traditions (Figures 2.2 and 2.3).

Obesity increases the risk of developing cardiovascular disease (CVD), certain types of cancer and Type 2 diabetes (Dixon, 2010). This last condition represents an epidemic in itself because of rapid increases in incidence, notably in young people (Narayan et al., 2003). Although obesity is not the only risk factor involved, there is a close relation by way of the metabolic syndrome – comprising central adiposity (fat around the abdomen), low levels of HDL or 'good' cholesterol, high levels of blood glucose and insulin, and hypertension (high blood pressure). Importantly, some studies find that the risk of CVD, hypertension and diabetes (at least) begins to rise at a body mass index (BMI; see Box 2.1) considerably below those that are conventionally used to define obesity or even overweight (Butland et al., 2007, p. 33). CVD, cancers, hypertension and Type 2 diabetes are the most frequent health concerns associated with obesity, but there are others. In the US, the prevalence of non-alcoholic fatty liver disease, closely associated with obesity, has more than doubled over the past two decades (O'Connor, 2014). Obesity also increases the risk of orthopaedic problems, sometimes requiring joint replacement, as people's joints simply cannot bear their weight; they were not designed to. These observations describe a connection between diseases and risk factors at a population level.

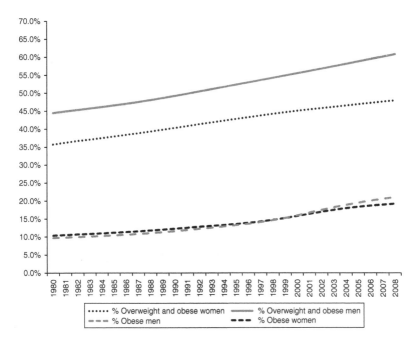

Figure 2.1 Percentage of the population that is overweight and obese, 1980–2008, in 21 countries

Notes: Obese = age standardized % population BMI ≥30, countries: Australia, Canada, Ireland, New Zealand, the UK, the US, Austria, Belgium, France, Germany, Italy, Japan, Switzerland, Netherlands, Denmark, Finland, Iceland, Sweden, Norway.
Overweight and Obese = age standardized % population BMI ≥25, countries as above except no data for Japan.
Source: Data adapted from Stevens et al. (2012).

There will usually be individuals within a population for whom the connection does not hold. In the context of overweight and obesity, these have been described in terms of the 'fat but fit', and the existence of a specific metabolic subtype unlikely to experience adverse health outcomes that would otherwise be expected has been postulated (Blüher, 2010). Whatever the explanations for the good health of such people, they are like the uncle or cousin (most people have one) who smoked like a chimney, drank half a bottle of whisky a day, and lived to 90. Such individuals exist, but their existence in no way undermines the strength of associations between risk factors and adverse health outcomes at a population level. The odds of being such a person are slim.

Box 2.1   Definitions of obesity and overweight

Among adults, obesity and overweight are usually defined with reference to the BMI. BMI is calculated by dividing a person's weight in kilograms divided by the square of his or her height in metres (kg/m^2). In adults, the World Health Organization (WHO) defines overweight as having a BMI greater than or equal to 25, and obesity as a BMI greater than or equal to 30. Among children, measurement is more complicated because of the need to adjust for changing body mass as children grow; a common definition of child and adolescent obesity involves a BMI in the top 5 per cent of distributions specified in child growth standards used by organizations like WHO or the US Centers for Disease Control and Prevention. BMI is somewhat contentious because of the possibility that it does not allow for normal differences in body mass among ethnic groups and may not be relevant to certain sub-populations such as professional athletes, but has the advantage of being easy to measure and relatively reliable as an indicator of trends over time within a population.

The importance of the obesity epidemic for population health is magnified by at least two further characteristics of the epidemic. First, in the high-income world a pronounced inverse socioeconomic gradient exists in the prevalence of obesity. In the US, a 2012 Institute of Medicine report noted that 'the burden of obesity is notably greater in racial/ethnic minority and low income populations' (Glickman et al., 2012). In other words, it is not a condition of affluence, but, rather, is more common among the poor and marginalized. For example, 42 per cent of US women living in households below the income level (130 per cent of the US official poverty line) that would make them eligible for federal food vouchers under the Supplemental Nutrition Assistance Program (SNAP – food stamps) in 2005–2008 were obese; among women in households with incomes above 350 per cent of the poverty line, the figure was 29 per cent. Among boys (age 2–19), the comparable figures were 21.1 per cent (for the lower-income group) and 11 per cent (for the relatively higher-income group) (Glickman et al., 2012). These figures may understate the economic gradient, since they do not separate out high-income populations – those with, say, household incomes five times or ten times the SNAP threshold. Although the overall rising trend in obesity appears to have flattened out in the US shortly after the

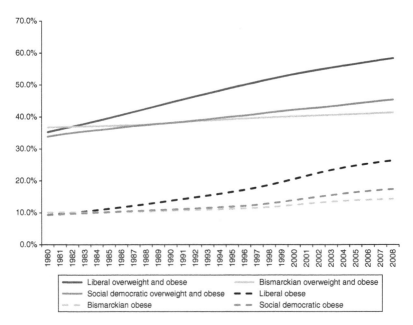

Figure 2.2 Percentage of women overweight and/or obese, 1980–2008, by welfare state regime

Notes:
1. Liberal countries are Australia, Canada, Ireland, New Zealand, the UK and the US.
2. Bismarckian countries are Austria, Belgium, France, Germany, Italy, Japan, Switzerland and the Netherlands.
3. Social democratic countries are Denmark, Finland, Iceland, Sweden and Norway.
4. Obese = age standardized % population BMI ≥30.
5. Overweight/obese = age standardized % population BMI ≥25; no data for Japan.
Source: Data adapted from Stevens et al. (2012).

start of the century, at least among adolescents socioeconomic disparities may be continuing to increase (Frederick et al., 2014), suggesting that in the future these will contribute to widening health inequalities. A similar pattern has been observed in England, where the socioeconomic gradient in obesity has been found to become steeper among school children between the time they enter school at age 4–5 and Year 6 (age 10–11), based on where the children's neighbourhood ranks in a national Index of Multiple Deprivation (IMD) that takes into account poverty rates, unemployment, service facilities and so forth (Hancock et al., 2013).

This finding is important because it demonstrates that the inverse socioeconomic gradient in obesity, like the gradient in many other adverse health outcomes, continues across the income spectrum, and is

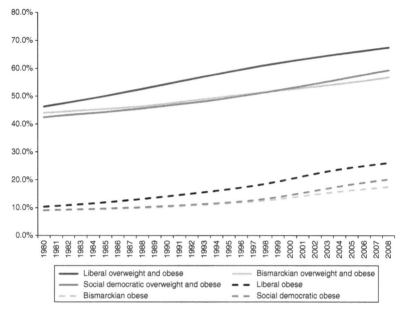

Figure 2.3   Percentage of men overweight and/or obese, 1980–2008, by welfare state regime

Notes:
1. Liberal countries are Australia, Canada, Ireland, New Zealand, the UK and the US.
2. Bismarckian countries are Austria, Belgium, France, Germany, Italy, Japan, Switzerland and the Netherlands.
3. Social democratic countries are Denmark, Finland, Iceland, Sweden and Norway.
4. Obese = age standardized % population BMI ≥30.
5. Overweight/obese = age standardized % population BMI ≥25; no data for Japan.
Source: Data adapted from Stevens et al. (2012).

not just confined to its lower reaches (a key finding from the Whitehall studies, which we discuss in more detail in Chapter 3). On a regional scale, leading obesity researcher Michael Goran and colleagues demonstrated a pronounced socioeconomic gradient in the prevalence of childhood and adolescent obesity among the 135 jurisdictions that comprise California's sprawling Los Angeles County, 'with a striking fourfold difference in childhood obesity prevalence between the communities with the highest and lowest levels of EH [economic hardship]' (Shih et al., 2013). A similar fourfold difference in obesity prevalence between the small areas (defined by postal code, or ZIP code as it is called in the US) with the lowest median residential property values and those with the highest was observed in a study of King County, Washington

State, which includes the city of Seattle (Drewnowski, 2012). Whether such relationships are driven by economic hardship as it operates at the individual level or by the relation between economic hardship and characteristics of the community is an ongoing debate in health social science, and the answer is probably: both, with the relative importance depending on the context (see Cummins et al., 2007).

Second, the obesity epidemic has spread far beyond the high-income world; it is a worldwide phenomenon (Malik et al., 2013; Popkin and Slining, 2013). Overweight and obesity are now rising rapidly in many middle- and some low-income countries as well, with prevalence in Mexican and Chilean adults comparable to levels in the US (Kain et al., 2014) and obesity seen as a crisis for both health and health care budgets by South Africa's health minister (Birrell, 2014). Similar rapid increases in obesity have been observed or anticipated in many other middle-income countries, notably in the Middle East (Kilpi et al., 2014). They are undergoing the *nutrition transition* – rapid urbanization, increasingly sedentary daily lives and a shift to highly processed diets containing high volumes of fats, sugars, meat, fish and dairy products – experienced in the high-income world, and in many cases that transition is occurring more rapidly (Popkin, 2002, 2007). 'The transition towards a high fat diet that took more than five decades in Japan has occurred in less than two in China' (Chopra and Darnton-Hill, 2004, p. 1558). As we show later in the chapter, explanations for the spread of obesity outside the high-income world make an important contribution to understanding this phenomenon as a neoliberal epidemic (Figure 2.1).

Causal complexity

When Tony Blair was the UK's prime minister, he said that many public health problems were 'not, strictly speaking, public health problems at all. They are questions of individual lifestyle – obesity, smoking, alcohol abuse, diabetes, sexually transmitted disease . . . These are not epidemics in the epidemiological sense – they are the result of millions of individual decisions, at millions of points in time' ('Blair calls', 2006). This is an extreme illustration of the behavioural, lifestyle-based perspective that people are simply making the wrong choices – eating unhealthy diets, drinking too much or not coping properly with stress. This perspective is increasingly at odds even with mainstream views in the health policy community. Thus, a web summary of a report on obesity by an expert panel of the US Institute of Medicine stated: 'The causes of the obesity epidemic are multifactorial, having much more to do with the absence of sidewalks and the limited availability of healthy and affordable foods than a lack of personal responsibility' (Institute of Medicine, 2012). Explanations that emphasize a combination of increased energy intake (through changes in diet) and reduced energy expenditure through physical activity are similarly unhelpful. They are unproblematic as far as they go, but also uninformative in terms of helping us to understand *why* the balance between energy intake and expenditure is changing. US researcher-activists Rodrick and Deborah Wallace (2005) argue that 'the "explanation" that "obesity occurs when people eat too much and get too little exercise" [is] in the same category as the remark by US President Calvin Coolidge...that "unemployment occurs when large numbers of people are out of work" '.

The challenge of explaining increases in overweight and obesity exemplifies the complexities we described in Chapter 1. This message of causal complexity has been emphasized by several recent expert panels in both the UK and the US (Kumanyika et al., 2002; Butland et al., 2007; Glickman et al., 2012). While genetic explanations focus on how human beings evolved to fatten rapidly as 'hunter-gatherers', when those carrying the genes in question would have been more likely to survive periods of scarcity and pass the relevant genes on to descendants (the 'thrifty genotype'), genetic variables cannot explain recent increases in overweight and obesity, which occurred over far too short a time period to reflect changes in the genotype. In other words, the increases must be attributable to changes in environmental variables, broadly defined. An incomplete inventory of these includes the food environment (including advertising, marketing, accessibility and affordability); the growth of sedentary work occupations and leisure time activity, such as television viewing; changing transport patterns, notably the rise of driving rather than walking; and changes in the built environment (Jones and Bentham, 2009). Each of these categories is complex, involving multiple variables and trends, some of which themselves demand explanation. For example, why has demand for convenient processed and pre-prepared foods increased, why has it been met with products that are high in sugars and fats and why have portion sizes increased (Young and Nestle, 2002; Fisher and Kral, 2008)? What accounts for increases in television viewing, which appears to have a causal connection with obesity (Gortmaker et al., 1996; Tremblay and Willms, 2003; Braithwaite et al., 2013), as a preferred leisure activity? Additional complexity is introduced by the possibility of causal influences that do not directly involve the balance between energy intake and energy expenditure; for example, environmental exposures, including those to endocrine-disrupting chemicals, may be altering metabolic functioning (Hatch et al., 2010; Casals-Casas and Desvergne, 2011). The obesity epidemic, in other words, has no single cause. Rather, it is necessary to think in terms of complex systems and multiple layers of explanation, within which the contribution of any particular variable is probably not discoverable through randomized controlled trials or quasi-experiments (Kumanyika et al., 2009). Furthermore, the relative importance of various environmental variables is likely to vary depending on the population in question – for example, children vs. adults or affluent vs. less affluent populations (Vandenbroeck et al., 2007a, 2007b; Glickman et al., 2012, pp. 7, 26). In the remainder of the chapter, we first apply the comparative perspective outlined in Chapter 1, using the concept of welfare state regimes, to the obesity epidemic. From the political economy perspective, we then explore in greater detail the reasons for thinking of obesity as a neoliberal epidemic.

Cross-national comparisons

Figures 2.2 and 2.3 show the rise of obesity (BMI $\geq$30) and overweight (BMI $\geq$25) for women and men by different welfare state regime during the period 1980–2008. There are clear time trends, with obesity and overweight increasing in all regimes rapidly during the 1980s and among both women and men. For example, in 1980 average obesity rates among men and women in the liberal welfare states were 10.4 and 9.3 per cent, respectively, while in the Bismarckian regime they were 9.1 and 10.1 per cent and in the social democratic countries they were 9.1 and 9.3 per cent. By 2008, average obesity rates had more than doubled in the liberal countries to 26 per cent for both men and women – meaning that more than a quarter of the adult population in these countries are obese. In the Bismarckian countries the increase was less pronounced, with 14.3 per cent of women and 17.5 per cent of men being obese in 2008. Similarly, increases in the social democratic countries were slower, with 17.4 per cent of women and 20.2 per cent of men being obese by 2008. The worst-performing high-income country in terms of obesity is the US.

These time trends in the rise of obesity and overweight in rich nations mirror the rise of neoliberalism, as shown in Figure 1.2 in Chapter 1. All countries experienced an increase in neoliberalism in the period 1980–2008, paralleled by an increase in obesity and overweight. Further, the countries which are currently the most neoliberal and experienced the greatest increases in neoliberalism during 1980–2008 – the liberal welfare state regimes – had correspondingly higher rates of obesity and overweight than the less neoliberal Bismarckian and social democratic countries. This shows that the timing and international spread of the obesity epidemic mirror the rise and diffusion of neoliberalism.

This phenomenon has been studied in more depth by De Vogli and colleagues (2014a), who analysed data for 127 countries from 1980 to 2008 and found that increases in BMI were significantly associated with economic globalization and income inequalities between and within countries (key characteristics of neoliberalism, as outlined in Chapter 1). A further analysis of 25 high-income countries between 1999 and 2008 found that the market deregulation policies associated with the rise of neoliberalism were associated with an increase in fast food consumption, which in turn increased mean BMI (De Vogli et al., 2014b). During the ten years studied, the average number of fast food transactions per year across the 25 countries increased by a fifth, from 27 per person in 1999 to 33 per person in 2008. Average BMI increased from 25.8 to 26.4 kg/m^2. The more deregulated countries had faster increases in both fast food consumption and BMI. Further, a study by Offer and colleagues (2010; reprinted as Offer et al., 2012) examined differences in obesity rates among welfare state regimes between 1994 and 2004. In keeping with the trends in Figures 2.2 and 2.3, they found that obesity rates were highest – and increased most rapidly – in the more liberal welfare states of Australia, Canada, the UK and (especially) the US. We explore some of the possible explanations in the section that follows.

Why a neoliberal epidemic?

We do not ascribe rapid increases in obesity solely to neoliberalism; the data show such increases even in countries where not only welfare regimes but also labour market policies can be characterized as social democratic. Rather, we argue that neoliberalism is a critical upstream influence, magnifying trends that are present to some extent throughout the high-income world.

Perhaps the most basic issue involves economic and social policies that mean many people cannot afford a healthy and balanced diet. As epidemiologist Adam Drewnowski has put it, 'Simply put, fats and sweets cost less, whereas many healthier foods cost more' (Drewnowski, 2009, p. S36). This problem obviously becomes more serious in circumstances when people lose jobs, are forced to take lower-paid jobs, or face cuts in income supports such as jobless or disability benefits. All these, as we show in later chapters, are defining features of neoliberalism, and have been especially significant in the US and the UK. To quote Drewnowski again, 'When incomes drop and family budgets shrink, food choices shift toward cheaper but more energy-dense foods. The first items dropped are usually healthier foods – high-quality proteins, whole grains, vegetables and fruit. Low cost energy-rich starches, added sugars, and vegetable fats represent the cheapest way to fill hungry stomachs' (Drewnowski and Eichelsdoerfer, 2010). In Canada's Ontario province, it would be arithmetically impossible for some categories of benefit recipients to afford a healthy diet if they were paying market rents for housing, even before a penny was spent on anything else (Association of Local Public Health Agencies, 2009); a more detailed study of living costs for benefit recipients in the smaller and poorer province of Nova Scotia found not only that eating a healthy diet was similarly unaffordable, but also that the problem had grown throughout the first decade of the new century (Williams et al., 2012). Healthy diets were becoming less and less affordable for the poor.

In the UK, 170 researchers and practitioners led by the president of the UK's Faculty of Public Health warned in 2014 about the health consequences of the increase in 'food poverty' associated with a 12 per cent real (i.e. inflation-adjusted) increase in food prices and a 7.6 per cent fall in average real hourly wages between 2008 and 2013 (Ashton et al., 2014). They did not directly address the further problem of cuts in benefits to those unable to work for various reasons, although a report that came out in the same year identified these cuts as being among the reasons for rapid increases in food bank usage (Cooper et al., 2014). Between 2002 and 2012, the price gap between a selection of 'more healthy' and 'less healthy' foods whose prices were recorded as background for the UK Consumer Price Index increased (Jones et al., 2014). Similar findings have been reported in local surveys in the US (e.g. Monsivais and Drewnowski, 2007; Monsivais et al., 2010). A US review of food price studies using market baskets (Horning and Fulkerson, 2015) reinforced the findings of earlier studies that food price estimates used to calculate the value of food stamps probably would not enable recipients to afford a healthy diet. Problems were also noted with how the market baskets were defined, 'including foods like white bread and rice, which are cheaper but less nutritious than their healthier counterparts' and 'may increase risk for becoming or remaining overweight/obese' (Horning and Fulkerson, 2015, p. 77). This observation is of particular concern because the number of food stamp recipients nearly doubled in the aftermath of the 2008 financial crisis, as noted in Chapter 4.

As disturbing as these figures are, estimates of the cost of healthy eating that fail to take into account what philosopher of science Jon

Elster has called the texture of everyday life understate the difficulty of eating a healthy diet while living on a low and/or precarious income, whether it is derived from benefits, from low-wage work or a combination. Access to stores that sell healthy food is the first problem. Especially in the US and parts of Canada, many low-income neighbourhoods and those with a high concentration of minority residents are 'food deserts' where there are few or no full service supermarkets or groceries, but abundant convenience stores where prices tend to be higher, and abundant fast food outlets (Beaulac et al., 2009; Treuhaft and Karpyn, 2010). Food deserts present special problems for people who do not own cars or have to economize on fuel, and who therefore are limited in their ability to shop for the lowest prices in a metropolitan landscape where public transport is often rudimentary or non-existent. In one such neighbourhood in downtown Halifax (Nova Scotia, Canada), a wheelchair-bound resident spends $20 he can ill afford on taxis every time he goes to the nearest supermarket; the taxis are a necessity because purchases in his wheelchair basket may otherwise be stolen (Beaumont, 2012). Studies of food deserts may further underestimate the difficulties of eating a healthy diet by neglecting 'food mirages': districts where there may be full service supermarkets, but with prices far beyond the reach of low-income residents (Breyer and Voss-Andreae, 2013).

Time poverty compounds the difficulties. When the demands of work (often on unpredictable schedules), transportation and (especially for women) child care are combined, not much time or energy are left for comparison shopping. Journalist Barbara Ehrenreich's narrative of her undercover venture into the low-wage service sector labour market (see Chapter 3) is eloquent on this point, as is an innovative 'geo-ethnography' (Matthews et al., 2005) of the lives of women pushed into the workforce by the US welfare 'reforms' of 1996 (discussed in more detail in Chapter 4). Matthews and colleagues described the hypothetical journey of one such woman – the description has to be hypothetical, because describing an actual journey might identify the research participant – as she leaves home at 6:30 am to walk to the day care centre and school to drop off her children before starting a bus journey of more than an hour to start work at 8:30 am. They note that '[t]he return journey home can be more complicated', for example if grocery shopping requires a detour involving a different bus route; the children must still be collected from school and day care. Many middle-class professionals, even buffered by higher incomes, would not have the energy to prepare healthy meals under these circumstances. Inadequacy of available cooking and food storage options presents another problem. Linda Tirado, whose experience of life on a low and precarious income provided the foundation for a best-selling book, explains:

> When I was pregnant the first time, I was living in a weekly motel for some time. I had a mini-fridge with no freezer and a microwave. I was on WIC [government-funded nutritional aid for women, infants and children]. I ate peanut butter from the jar and frozen burritos because they were 12 for $2. Had I had a stove, I couldn't have made beef burritos that cheaply.... Broccoli is intimidating. You have to have a working stove, and pots, and spices, and you'll have to do the dishes no matter how tired you are or they'll attract bugs.
>
> (Tirado, 2014)

Across low-, middle- and high-income countries, a strong correlation exists between the consumption of packaged food per person and levels of sugar consumption and obesity, although with considerable variation at any given level of packaged food consumption (Figure 2.4). In 2004, Chopra and Darnton-Hill pointed out a resemblance between the epidemics of smoking and obesity: both involve the activities of large transnational corporations (in cigarette production, food processing and marketing and fast food) with massive budgets for research and marketing. Indeed, sometimes the same companies are involved, using similar marketing strategies: from 1985 to 1988, Nabisco (producer of Oreo cookies) was owned by tobacco giant R.J. Reynolds (Camel cigarettes), and Philip Morris (Marlboro cigarettes) acquired General Foods in 1985 and Kraft in 1988. It has been argued that the 'ultra-processed' food and drink industry, along with the alcohol industry, is responsible for an 'industrial epidemic' of non-communicable diseases (NCDs): 'In industrial epidemics, the vectors of spread are not biological agents, but transnational corporations' (Moodie et al., 2013, p. 671). Thus, the obesity epidemic can be seen in part as a logical result of a policy environment in which provision of a basic necessity has been converted into a highly profitable business, where profit is dependent on increasing consumption of high-margin products that are inexpensive to produce. Ultra-processed products 'made from processed substances extracted or refined from whole foods' and designed for 'intense palatability (achieved by high content of fat, sugar, salt, and cosmetic and other additives)' (Monteiro et al., 2013, p. 22) are central to achieving this objective. High-fructose corn syrup (HFCS), thought by some researchers to play a significant role in the rising incidence of diabetes (Goran et al., 2013), and processed cheese (Moss, 2013,

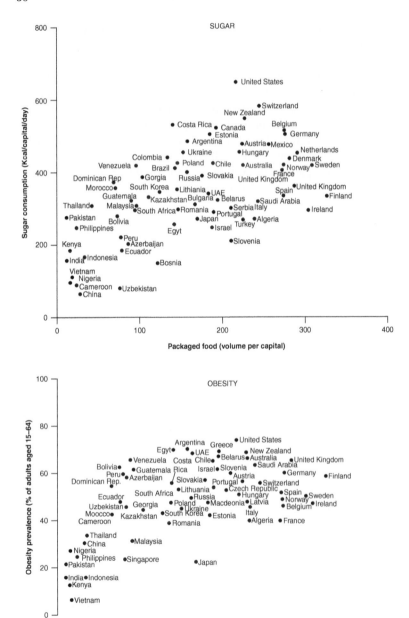

Figure 2.4 Association of packaged food volume (per capita) with sugar consumption and obesity prevalence, 2005

Source: Stuckler, D., McKee, M., Ebrahim, S., and Basu, S. (2012b) 'Manufacturing Epidemics: The Role of Global Producers in Increased Consumption of Unhealthy Commodities Including Processed Foods, Alcohol, and Tobacco.' *PLoS Med, 9*, e1001235. Reproduced under an Unrestricted Creative Commons Licence.

pp. 160–177) are two examples of such substances. The food industry invests heavily in research to improve 'intense palatability', now including the use of brain scans, and in marketing efforts that often target children (Moss, 2013; Freudenberg, 2014, pp. 100–112). In 2012, it was estimated that US children see more than 1000 fast food television commercials per year, with McDonald's alone accounting for a fifth or more of these (Feloni, 2013); the effectiveness of such advertising in influencing children's brand and dietary preferences is well established (Andreyeva et al., 2011; Cornwell et al., 2014). The percentage of 'total purchased calories' that Canadians obtained from ultra-processed products more than doubled between 1938 and 2001, from 24.4 to 54.9 per cent (Monteiro et al., 2013, p. 14).

Resisting regulation is also part of the picture, as 'corporate disease vectors implement sophisticated campaigns to undermine public health interventions' (Moodie et al., 2013, p. 671). A detailed 2012 journalistic exposé described a campaign of this kind by the US sugar industry, going back to 1942 (Taubes and Couzens, 2012). Central to the campaign was a strategy that David Michaels, a former US assistant secretary of energy for environment, safety and health, has called 'manufacturing uncertainty' (Michaels and Monforton, 2005; Michaels, 2006) through the selective use and support of scientific research – a strategy that was perfected by the tobacco and asbestos industries. Rather than acting to protect public health, governments are often actively involved in promoting the interests of the industry. An extreme example of the mind-set in question, although it does not relate to obesity but, rather, to the practice of allowing suppliers of ground beef to self-regulate rather than mandating testing for bacterial contamination, was supplied by an official of the US Department of Agriculture in 2009: 'I have to look at the entire industry, not just what is best for public health' (Moss, 2009). In Canada, members of federal government advisory committees often have direct financial ties to the food industry, which may explain the government's hands-off approach even to such basics as ensuring the accuracy of nutritional labelling (Campbell et al., 2013). A related strategy involves the promotion of voluntary codes of practice, although in the case of marketing to children academic research – in contrast to the industry's own studies – has shown these to be of limited effectiveness (Galbraith-Emami and Lobstein, 2013). In the UK, the Conservative-led government opted to address obesity by way of a so-called Public Health Responsibility Deal that actively involved representatives of the food, supermarket and restaurant industries (Panjwani and Caraher, 2014); this was one of several such deals, with others involving the alcohol and tobacco industries. In July 2013, the Faculty of Public Health (the national college of public health specialists) withdrew from all the deals, citing in particular the government's refusal to introduce plain packaging for cigarettes or a minimum unit price for alcohol. Although research on this topic is scarce, it appears that the food industry has been active in resisting regulation at the international level, as well. In advance of the 2011 United Nations Summit on NCDs, some observers claimed that transnational corporations, including those in the food processing industry, were shaping the negotiating positions of high-income countries in pre-conference drafting sessions where the real negotiation took place (Cohen, 2011; Stuckler et al., 2011).

A more direct link with neoliberalism involves the expansion of the food industry into lower- and middle-income countries (LMICs), whose growing economies offer attractive possibilities for expansion. In countries as diverse as Brazil, Mexico, India, Russia and South Africa, many of the same transnational corporations that dominate the packaged food industry in the United States are prominent (Stuckler et al., 2012b). In Brazil, ultra-processed products increased as a proportion of purchased food from 18.7 per cent in 1987 to 26.1 per cent in 2003 (Monteiro et al., 2013, p. 23). The growth of three categories of ultra-processed products in middle-income countries as a whole is shown in Table 2.1. If the process is driven by the food industry's need for new markets, as those in the high-income world approach saturation despite such phenomena as supersizing (Young and Nestle, 2002; Young and Nestle, 2007; Fisher and Kral, 2008), it is facilitated by trade and investment treaties that open markets to foreign investment. Epidemiologist David Stuckler and colleagues (2012b) found a strong correlation between the level of foreign investment as a percentage of GDP and 'greater exposure to unhealthy food commodities, especially for soft

Table 2.1 Annual growth rate in per capita retail sales of selected products, 1998–2012

	Upper-middle-income countries	Lower-middle-income countries
Frozen products	6.01%	7.67%
Snacks	2.79%	5.45%
Soft drinks	2.83%	9.90%

Source: Data from Monteiro et al. (2013).

drinks, processed foods and alcohol' across 50 LMICs. Even more strikingly, LMICs that have trade agreements with the US have per capita levels of soft-drink consumption more than 50 per cent higher than those that do not (Stuckler et al., 2012a). A 2012 article on 'exporting obesity' (Clark et al., 2012) argues that the combination of farm subsidies in the US and the removal of trade and investment barriers between the US and Mexico under the North American Free Trade Agreement (NAFTA) led to rapid transformation of the Mexican food system in several respects. US agricultural exports to Mexico have increased rapidly, as has the penetration into Mexico of US transnationals such as McDonald's and Wal-Mart.

A specific illustration of the relevance of trade liberalization involves the rapid growth of US exports of subsidized corn to Mexico, partly in the form of HFCS, after a 2006 World Trade Organization dispute settlement ruling that invalidated a Mexican tax on soft drinks sweetened with anything other than cane sugar (Goran et al., 2013). Ironically, the agricultural subsidy programs that enable US exports to underprice Mexican producers remain permissible under the current trade law regime, and the US has doggedly resisted efforts to end them. A similar analysis has been developed with reference to trade liberalization in Central America, where the volume of many categories of food imports from the US increased severalfold between 1990 and 2006 (Thow and Hawkes, 2009). More generally, researchers have linked liberalization of trade and investment to the acceleration of the nutrition transition in LMICs (Hawkes et al., 2009), and expressed special concern that new, far-reaching multilateral agreements such as the proposed Trans-Pacific Partnership (TPP) Agreement will further limit the scope for national efforts to address the obesity epidemic (Thow et al., 2014). Such agreements go far beyond lowering barriers to trade at national borders, to address such issues as domestic regulatory requirements and labour standards.

Another connection with neoliberalism was explored at a groundbreaking workshop at the University of Oxford in 2009 (Offer et al., 2012). The common theme of the presentations, drawn from multiple disciplines, was that political structures such as welfare regimes influence the obesity epidemic. More specifically, higher levels of economic insecurity – associated with market liberalism and the 'creative destruction' that Joseph Schumpeter extolled as a defining virtue of capitalism – are causally linked with a higher prevalence of obesity (Wisman and Capehart, 2012). Drewnowski, whom we have quoted earlier, was more explicit: 'Arguably, the social and economic policies of the past several decades have created an economic underclass that is increasingly obese and diabetic' (Drewnowski, 2012, p. 83). The research that laid the foundations for this conclusion was not new. For example, at least as long ago as 1999, it was hypothesized that a socioeconomic gradient in sleep deprivation might be responsible for increasing the risk of obesity and diabetes (Van Cauter and Spiegel, 1999); it is not hard to make the connection with such variables as multiple job-holding, irregular hours, and the demands of balancing work and domestic responsibilities. More recent research has added support for this explanation (Bray and Young, 2012). Also at the end of the 1990s, the Whitehall II study of health inequalities among British civil servants, which we discuss at greater length in Chapter 3, found that people whose jobs were threatened by restructuring were more likely to experience increases in BMI and several other adverse health outcomes than colleagues whose jobs remained secure, after controlling for other factors (Ferrie et al., 1998).

But why would economic insecurity lead to obesity? As with the causes of obesity more generally, the plausible pathways are multiple, and likely to vary in importance depending on the specific population in question. One involves what Offer et al. (2012) call the 'fast-food shock': the declining price and increasing convenience, accompanied of course by intensive marketing, of products like the Big Mac. More general material explanations involve the combination of affordability issues and time pressure described earlier. As Linda Tirado put it, 'Convenience food is just that. And we', that is, the poor and economically insecure, 'are not allowed many conveniences.' Another involves the psychosocial pathway of what might be called eating for solace or compensation (Pickett and Wilkinson, 2012, pp. 186–188).

Perhaps the best-supported explanation, though, involves physiological pathways related to stress – a concept that has multiple colloquial meanings, but one that is measurable in biological terms using the concept of allostatic load (McEwen, 1998). We explore stress and its relation to insecurity and inequality in more depth in chapters 3 (with a major emphasis on work and employment) and 5 (with a more general focus on inequality). Here, the critical points are as follows. First, stress can be related not only to insecurity but also to subordinate position in a hierarchy, as in the case of the thoroughly hierarchical British civil service that was the topic of the Whitehall studies, and to the overall level of inequality in a society (Pickett and Wilkinson, 2012). Second, stress 'may have direct physiological effects that influence weight change, *and* indirect effects on weight change mediated by health behaviours, including diet and physical activity' (Bell et al., 2012, p. 117, emphasis added). Third, what epidemiologists call psychosocial or behavioural and material explanations cannot be separated, since one's socioeconomic position also has important consequences for one's opportunities to eat a healthy diet and be physically active.

If a community has no safe places to walk or play, lacks food outlets offering affordable healthy foods, and is bombarded by advertisements for unhealthy foods and beverages, its residents will have less opportunity to engage in physical activity and eating behaviors that allow them to achieve and maintain a healthy weight.

(Institute of Medicine, 2012)

Fourth, and more generally, the various explanations for a connection between insecurity and obesity *are not competing or mutually exclusive.* Our greatest concern is with how neoliberalism tends to concentrate both advantage and adversity in ways that lead to adverse health outcomes and widening health inequalities. That is the topic of the rest of the book.

3

Insecurity: How Politics Gets Under Our Skin

In this chapter we focus on the neoliberal epidemic of insecurity. Here we argue that neoliberalism has made the labour market and the world of work far less secure and consequently more stressful and health damaging. This insecurity manifests itself through reductions in workplace rights, job security, pay levels and welfare rights (so-called flexibility). We argue that this has led to large increases in chronic stress across the populations of many countries (and particularly in the most vulnerable groups), resulting in a myriad of chronic diseases, including musculoskeletal pain and cardiovascular disease. International comparisons are made with countries that have taken a less neoliberal political path.

Neoliberalism and the rise of insecurity

On the morning of 25 August 2014 a young New Jersey woman, Maria Fernandes, died from inhaling gasoline fumes as she slept in her 13-year-old car. She often slept in the car while shuttling between her three low-wage jobs in food service, and kept a can of gasoline in the car because she often slept with the engine running, and was worried about running out of gasoline. Apparently, the can accidentally tipped over and the vapours from spilled gasoline cost her life (Swarns, 2014). Ms Fernandes' death can also be attributed to transformations in labour markets that have been a key feature of neoliberalism over the past few decades – indeed, at least until the financial crisis of 2008, its most visible and dramatic manifestation in the high-income world. For increasing numbers of people in many countries, especially those that have travelled farthest down the neoliberal path, the transformation has turned the idea of a job that provides adequate income and security into an unattainable dream (Goos and Manning, 2007; Kalleberg, 2011).

The connections between labour market transformations and poor health operate through multiple pathways, of which the one exemplified by Ms Fernandes' death is only the most dramatic. The two most extensive reviews of scientific evidence on how new forms of work organization worldwide have affected health found a clear link between 'precarious' or 'downsized' employment and work-related illness and injury (Quinlan et al., 2001; Quinlan and Bohle, 2009). Around the turn of the millennium, journalists Barbara Ehrenreich and Polly Toynbee 'went undercover' in the US and the UK, respectively, to explore the day-to-day realities of the expanded low-wage, insecure service sector labour market that was and is a key element of those transformations (Ehrenreich, 2001; Toynbee, 2003). They described the physically demanding nature of the work and associated exposures to low-grade workplace hazards; the constant struggle to find affordable housing and the frequent unaffordability of a healthy diet, complicated by the time-consuming logistics of being poor (especially in the US context of non-existent public transport); and the particular demands of combining all these with child care and (again in the US context) lack of health insurance. Their work is a powerful reminder of how neoliberalism operates through labour markets to undermine health not only by way of the material consequences of unemployment or inadequate employment, as important and neglected as these are, but also through chronic exposure to stress that 'gets under your skin' by way of multiple biological mechanisms. These are sometimes described as psychosocial, but the appropriateness of this term can be questioned, since the relevant physiology is relatively well understood, and the implication that the issues are 'in people's heads' is thoroughly misleading.

In this chapter we first describe in greater detail the politics of labour market transformations in the two countries that are our focus, and then outline the scientific evidence base for the connection of labour market insecurity, stress and health. We conclude with a comparative focus on health, insecurity and social policy.

How political choices have led to an epidemic of insecurity

The transformation of labour markets that led to the exposures we have described began in the 1970s. Corporate managers began to shift labour-intensive production in some industries, such as semiconductors and garment manufacturing, to lower-wage locations in low- and middle-income countries (LMICs). Often, these were export processing zones (EPZs) established by the governments of those countries specifically to attract foreign investment with the lure of tax breaks, no tariffs on imports of raw materials for export production, extremely low wages, 'flexible' employment relations, and little or no regulation of working conditions (Fröbel et al., 1980; Ross, 1997). Technological innovation underpinned this global reorganization of production (Marchak, 1991); think not only about advances in information and communications technology but also about such developments as the containerization of shipping. Reorganization was later accelerated by the incorporation of India, China and the economies of the former Soviet bloc into global trade and investment flows, which roughly doubled the size of the world's labour force (Freeman, 2007) – itself the outcome of a complex set of political choices. Statistically, the earliest and most conspicuous result was a dramatic decline in the importance of manufacturing employment throughout the high-income world, which a recent analysis finds to be an important contributor to overall increases in levels of unemployment (Kollmeyer and Pichler, 2013). As an indication of the extent of geographic shifts in the location of production and their connection with employment and income, by 2008 there were more than twice as many manufacturing workers in China (99 million) as in all the G7 countries combined, but the workers in those factories were earning US$1.36 an hour on average – approximately 4 per cent of hourly compensation costs in US manufacturing and 3 per cent of those in the Euro area (Banister and Cook, 2011).

Manufacturing employment is important in at least four other respects. First, national statistics on the decline of manufacturing employment fail to capture the far more serious localized impacts of such 'deindustrialization' (Bluestone and Harrison, 1982). Some cities in the US that had historically relied on manufacturing lost more than half of their total employment base within a relatively short period (Schrecker et al., 2012). The city of Detroit, once the centre of the North American auto industry, exemplifies the consequences, with its municipal government bankrupt and a population smaller than in 1910 and less than half its size in 1970 (Davey, 2013; Uberti, 2014). Many regions in the UK that had formerly been prosperous crucibles of industrialization, including the North East where we live and work, suffered comparable declines (see e.g. Beynon et al., 1994; the deindustrialization of the North is discussed again in Chapter 5). Even in London, as recently as 1961 a third of workers were employed in manufacturing (Wills et al., 2010, p. 32); today that number is minuscule. Second, many of the jobs in question had historically been accessible to those with limited formal qualifications – leading researchers who should know better to characterize them, inaccurately, as 'unskilled' (Nickell and Bell, 1995). These jobs provided important access to adequate incomes for many people who now have no comparable options. Third, manufacturing workplaces were, and in some jurisdictions still are, highly unionized – making them at the same time a bastion and a target. Fourth, in contrast to the organization of work around mass production, it can be argued that the service sector – which has expanded rapidly throughout the high-income world – involves inherent tendencies to a wider dispersion of earnings, and is more amenable to the informalization of work and the growth of low-wage, precarious employment (Sassen, 2002).

On this point, not only the kinds of jobs but also the ways they are organized have changed considerably over the past few decades, with a decline in the number of standard full-time, permanent jobs and a sharp increase in flexible or precarious employment: more and more people are working on either temporary contracts or no contracts, with limited or no employment or welfare rights. In this new economy, skills, working hours, contracts, conditions, pay and location are all more flexible and precarious. The once standard full-time, permanent contract with benefits has been superseded by a number of atypical forms of employment which tend to be characterized by lower levels of security and poorer working conditions (Benach et al., 2002). Rather than being a transitory stage in an individual's employment history, atypical forms of labour are becoming the norm for many workers in the labour force of advanced capitalist economies (Virtanen et al., 2002). In an important ethnographic study of Teesside, a formerly prosperous Northern manufacturing region that is now among the most deprived in England, Shildrick et al. (2012b, p. 59) observed: 'Moving in and out of jobs, and above and below the poverty line, over a working life is...now the normal experience for many working-class people.' This 'low-pay, no-pay cycle' is not an idiosyncratically chosen example, but, rather, an instance of an international trend that economist Guy Standing, who worked for more than 25 years at the International Labour Organization, has described as the emergence of a new stratum of workers he calls the precariat (Standing, 2014). An alternative description refers to 'the swelling ranks of the employed but exposed' (Clark and Heath, 2014, pp. 80–88). The expansion of the precariat is exemplified by what are called zero-hours contracts in the UK, under which workers have no set hours of work and are not guaranteed even minimum hours from week to week.

Such contracts also reduce entitlements to certain out-of-work benefits, and to pensions. In 2014, 1.4 million workers in the UK were on such contracts (Seymour, 2014). These contracts are extensively used by large multinational companies such as Amazon, which have also been criticized for paying very little UK cooperation tax (BBC News, 2013). Across the European Union, temporary, insecure work accounted for an average of around 15 per cent of paid employment (an average of 16.4 per cent in the EU-15 countries and an average of 14 per cent in the EU-27 countries) before the impact of the financial crisis (Massarelli, 2009). This amounts to 19.1 million full-time temporary workers. Directly comparable data for the US are hard to find, but the number of involuntary part-time workers (those who want full-time work but cannot find it) rose from 5.7 million in 2000 to 8.9 million in 2010 (Mishel et al., 2012, p. 350), and the number of people employed through temporary help agencies doubled (to 2.7 million) between 1993 and 2013 (Clark and Heath, 2014, p. 85). Temporary work is considerably more prevalent among women than men, and among the young and immigrant populations. The gains to employers from such job insecurity include lower wages and lower associated costs such as pensions or sickness benefits: or, put more simply, higher profits. However, these benefits to employers are accompanied by adverse consequences for workers, with precarious employment characterized by low incomes, long and unpredictable hours, and (for many women) the ongoing challenge of combining work and child care (see e.g. Heymann, 2006; Ruan and Reichman, 2014). Another consequence with important implications for public policy is that most workers on involuntary part-time jobs, or on zero-hours contracts, are still counted as 'employed' for statistical purposes, thus understating the effects of neoliberalism on employment.

Although the decline of manufacturing has been evident throughout the high-income world, other transformations of labour markets have unfolded unevenly. In the two countries with which we are most concerned, the UK and the US, it is especially important to see such patterns as deindustrialization and the expansion of the precariat as the outcome of conscious decisions to pursue neoliberal agendas, as they are accompanied by the abandonment of the pursuit of full employment – once a pillar of political and economic policy, especially in the UK until 1979 (Bambra, 2011).

The monetarist pursuit of low inflation by the Thatcher and Reagan governments accepted high unemployment and its social consequences as collateral damage. Norman Lamont, the Conservative UK chancellor of the exchequer (finance minister) stated in 1991 that 'rising unemployment and the recession have been the price that we have had to pay to get inflation down. That price is well worth paying' (House of Commons, 1991). This was echoed in 1998 by Eddie George, then governor of the Bank of England, who stated that 'northern unemployment is an acceptable price to pay for curbing southern inflation' (BBC News, 1998). In Chapter 5, we examine some of the consequences of this spatially uneven distribution of the collateral damage from neoliberalization. Testifying before Congress in 1997, US Federal Reserve head Alan Greenspan commented that

> Atypical restraint on compensation increases has been evident for a few years now and appears to be mainly the consequence of greater worker insecurity, possibly owing to the rapid evolution of technologies in use in the workplace. Technological change almost surely has been an important impetus behind corporate restructuring and downsizing. Also, it contributes to the concern of workers that their job skills may become inadequate.
>
> (US House of Representatives, 1997, p. 28)

It is important to emphasize that he saw this level of insecurity as a good thing.

Labour market policies in both the US and the UK post-1979 involved attacks on the trade unions and labour standards that historically have been the main protectors of wage levels and working conditions. In the UK, legal changes initiated by the Thatcher government drastically reduced the ability of unions to organize and bargain collectively (Brown et al., 1997). The militarized response to the miners' strike was the most visible element of this strategy (Milne, 2004), but it was paralleled by a wave of privatizations that had the effect of further reducing union power (see Figure 3.1), increasing the exposure of British manufacturing to international competition. Meanwhile, the Thatcher government and all subsequent governments emphasized the financial services industry as the basis for economic growth strategies. The result was a massive shift of corporate investment offshore. Geographer Ray Hudson notes that 'Between 1979 and 1986 the UK's 40 largest manufacturing firms increased their non-UK employment by 125,000 while cutting employment in the UK by 415,000' (Hudson, 2013, p. 378). By the 1990s the newly de-unionized environment, in which average hourly manufacturing compensation was 22 Deutschmarks as against 44 in Germany and 36 in Japan, was increasingly attractive to foreign investors (Stevenson, 1995), but even the *Wall Street Journal* conceded that the new jobs were poorly paid, and emphasized

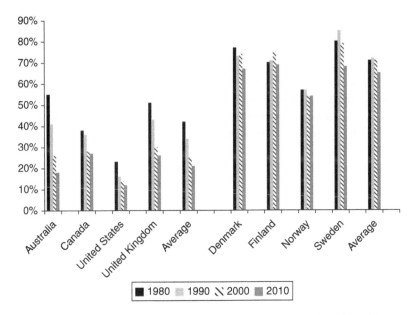

Figure 3.1   Trends in trade union density as a percentage of paid workforce, 1980–2010, in selected liberal and social democratic countries
Source: OECD (2014), http://stats.oecd.org/Index.aspx?DataSetCode=UN_DEN and Visser, J. (1990) 'Key Issues for Labour Market and Social Policies: Trends in Trade Union Membership', in OECD *Employment Outlook* (Paris: OECD), http://www.oecd.org/els/emp/4358365 .pdf (accessed 20 November 2014).

the importance of 'more flexible' labour relations in attracting investment (Milbank, 1994). Famously, Labour prime minister Tony Blair campaigned on a promise to 'leave British law the most restrictive on trade unions in the Western world' (quoted in Howell, 2005, p. 176).

In the US, the Reagan government's firing of striking air traffic controllers in 1981 is sometimes seen as a watershed, but the nature of US political institutions – and the extent of state-level variation in industrial relations regimes – meant that the neoliberal transformation of labour markets unfolded more slowly and unevenly. As long ago as the 1970s, so-called right-to-work laws, which prohibit the closed shop[5] and impose various other restrictions on worker organization (Collins, 2012), had drawn the attention of Japanese investors:

> Southern wages were noticeably lower than the national average, and unions were rare. . . . All southern states except Kentucky had right-to-work laws on the books. Compared to the loaded packages commonly

provided to the Japanese workforce, the bare-bones expectations of nonunion American labor regarding fringe benefits meant significant savings for prospective Japanese employers.

(Guthrie-Shimizu, 2005, pp. 143–144)

Both domestic and foreign investment shifted to the right-to-work south east, in part as a response to Reagan-era federal defence procurement decisions (Markusen et al., 1991). Meanwhile, the real (inflation-adjusted) value of the federal minimum wage declined from US$8.38 (in 2011 dollars) in 1979 to a low point of $5.87 in 1989, and after increases in 2007 and 2008 was still only $7.25, actually below its level as long ago as 1967, and the number of workers covered by higher state minimum wages declined (Mishel et al., 2012, pp. 279–286). More recently, in what can fairly be characterized as a race to the bottom, two northern states, Michigan and Indiana, have adopted southern-style right-to-work laws in efforts to attract direct investment. Meanwhile, localized anti-union efforts by employers proliferated in a permissive legal environment (Milkman, 2008; Kalleberg, 2011, pp. 31–34). The decline of union membership in the US private sector has been precipitous, from almost 25 per cent among private sector workers in 1973 – already low in comparison with other high-income countries – to 13 or 14 per cent, depending on the source, in 2009. This was, in fact, a manifestation of a general trend – '[in] the nineteen non-Scandinavian [high-income] countries, trade union density between 1970 and 2007 declined from just under 40 percent to 23 percent' (Scharpf, 2013, p. 179), but the impact on incomes and employment relations was far less severe in jurisdictions that (for example) extend coverage of collective agreements even to non-union workers or offer strong minimum wage protections... and, in the Scandinavian countries, union density and collective bargaining coverage remained high (Figure 3.1).

A further element of the policy landscape, especially in the US but with important spillover effects because of the size of the country's economy and the reach of its transnational corporations, involved changes in capital markets and corporate decision-making that arose from the combination of recession (at the end of the 1970s) and the growing market power of institutional investors (pension funds, mutual funds and more recently hedge funds) concerned almost entirely with short-term increases in share prices (Useem, 1996; Madrick, 2012). Indicative of the impact on economic priorities is the cover of a 2003 issue of *Fortune* magazine that showed pictures of the chief executives of four major US firms; an accompanying article cheered: 'The four companies whose CEOs are on the cover of this magazine have shed upwards of 250,000 jobs under their present leaders while creating $104 billion of new wealth' (Sherman, 1993). The author meant shareholder wealth, of course; the workers whose wealth had been diminished by the job cuts were conveniently forgotten. News headlines during the 1990s routinely announced cuts of thousands of jobs by corporations that were already profitable, but seeking to boost their attractiveness to investors; between 1992 and 1995, just ten US firms had cut almost half a million jobs (Kirk, 1995). Terms like downsizing, outsourcing (contracting out parts of the production process) and more recently offshoring became part of the everyday vocabulary (Uchitelle et al., 1996; Milberg, 2004; Grossman and Rossi-Hansberg, 2006); so did downward mobility (Newman, 1988). Although jobs were being created at the same time, they were hardly replacements but, rather, low-wage and precarious jobs in the service sector – the kinds of jobs that Ehrenreich and Toynbee were able to find, and the kind that now sustain an expanding proportion of the population in the countries they investigated, and in others.

The trends described are not inevitable, and reflect (among other influences) national, politically chosen differences in labour market policy. A major comparative study of Denmark, France, Germany, the Netherlands, the UK and the US (Gautié and Schmitt, 2010) found that in the mid-2000s low-wage work, defined as work that paid less than two-thirds the gross hourly median wage, was three times as common in the US as in Denmark, and twice as common as in France. Movement towards the US norm was clearly evident over the 1980–2005 period in some countries, such as the UK and post-reunification Germany, but not in others, although the countries in question had 'all been exposed over the last several decades to the same increases in globalization, technology, and competition within national product markets' (Appelbaum et al., 2010, p. 5). As in other studies, there was a clear and unsurprising correlation with rates of unionization and collective bargaining coverage, with 82 per cent of Dutch and Danish workers covered by collective agreements, as against the US figure of 14 per cent (Bosch et al., 2010).

The labour market transformations we have described are best thought of as an element of what political scientist Jacob Hacker (2008), writing in the US context, has described as 'the great risk shift': a process in which labour market transformations and welfare state retrenchment combine both to increase economic uncertainty and to shift responsibility for dealing with it from employers (via secure employment and funded pensions) and governments (via social safety nets like unemployment compensation) to individuals and households.

As one illustration, the chance that working-age Americans would experience a drop of 50 per cent or more in income from one year to the next more than doubled between the early 1970s and the end of the century (Hacker, 2008, p. 31). For Hacker, other indications included rising personal bankruptcy and mortgage foreclosure rates; insecurity in retirement, as defined-benefit pensions were replaced by defined-contribution plans, sometimes (as in the infamous case of Enron employees) invested in high-risk assets; and insecurity in illness, as the market-driven US health care industry systematically failed those who needed it most. On the other hand, literally trillions of dollars were mobilized in short order to bail out financial institutions that had been permitted to become too big to fail. From our political economy perspective, the great risk shift is a defining characteristic of neoliberalism, as it redistributes income and wealth upward in society while redistributing risk downward – privatizing it (Hacker, 2004) to be dealt with by individuals and households. We describe two further dimensions of this process in the remainder of the chapter. First, we expand on the argument that the great risk shift can be hazardous to your health, in ways that go beyond access to health care and the material deprivations of inadequate income. Second, we provide some cross-national comparisons of how those hazards differ across welfare regimes in the high-income world.

How neoliberalism gets under our skin

These new forms of labour market structure and work organization affect our health in various ways, partly through their direct material consequences on income levels and volatility but also, and relatedly, by increasing levels of chronic stress within the population. Stress gets under your skin in multiple ways that affect health. At a biological level, exposure to stress stimulates both the sympathetic–adrenomedullary and the hypothalamic–pituitary–adrenocortical systems (Bartley, 2004). Brunner (1997) uses the 'fight or flight' evolutionary response to stress to explain the biological mechanisms underpinning the body's reactions to psychosocial stressors. When the body perceives stress, in the form of an adverse environmental trigger, the sympathetic–adrenomedullary pathway is stimulated with the rapid release of adrenaline and noradrenaline. These neurotransmitters orchestrate a cascade of physiological events including, among other changes, increases in blood pressure, heart rate and the release of energy resources (Brunner, 1997). Originally this response would have been adaptive in that it would have enabled the individual to retreat from the stressor or to fight back. In society today, however, such 'fight or flight' responses may not be possible (e.g. if the stressor is poor relations at work or stigmatization of your social group by the media), so the response ends up being suppressed. In addition, the hypothalamic–pituitary–adrenocortical system is stimulated. In simple terms, this results in the release of cortisol, a glucocorticoid hormone, which has multiple physiological effects, including the release of energy resources, suppression of the immune system and direct effects on mood (Brunner, 1997). The process of cortisol secretion involves communication between the hypothalamus and the pituitary gland (both located in the lower central part of the brain) to cause the release of adrenocorticotropic hormone in response to a stress stimulus. Adrenocorticotropic hormone subsequently induces the production and release of cortisol from the adrenal cortex (of the adrenal glands) into the blood (Bartley, 2004).

Brunner (1997) explains that activation of both the sympathetic–adrenomedullary and the hypothalamic–pituitary–adrenocortical systems is likely to be socially patterned, with differences in the magnitude and length of responses being related to individual coping resources and differential exposures to adverse environmental factors. The prolonged activation of the autonomic nervous system and neuroendocrine systems ('stress') is likely to result in reduced biological resilience over time, with measurable health consequences. The most widely used indicator of the physiological effects is allostatic load, 'the wear and tear that results' from that prolonged activation (McEwen, 1998). Allostatic load can be measured using various indicators that are commonly gathered in population health surveys and longitudinal epidemiological studies to generate allostatic load scores that have been found to predict increased risk for cardiovascular disease, among other adverse outcomes (McEwen and Seeman, 2009), and research in both human beings and primate populations continues to expand understandings of the consequences of stress and its relation to socioeconomic position or, in non-human species, position in social hierarchies (McEwen, 2012; Marmot and Sapolsky, 2014). In two especially striking studies described in more detail in Chapter 5, allostatic load scores were used to assess the biological 'weathering' effects associated with subordinate racial and gender status. In addition to the direct effects of stress, via biological responses to stress triggers, the effects of stress on health operate indirectly through changes to health-related behaviours, such as modifications to smoking patterns, alcohol consumption, dietary intake or participation in physical activity (Martikainen et al.,

2004). We are cautious about placing too much emphasis on this pathway as it applies to entire national populations, because it can be difficult to identify the component of such changes that represents a behavioural response to stress that is independent of material constraints.

The prevalence of stress and stress-related illnesses has increased over time. For example, a US study found that rates of stress increased by 18 per cent for women and 24 per cent for men between 1983 and 2009 (Cohen and Janicki-Deverts, 2012). Similarly, there is evidence to indicate that stress-related disorders such as depression and anxiety have also increased during the neoliberal era, with, for example, antidepressant medication usage rising fourfold in the USA between 1988 and 2008, with more than 10 per cent of the population now receiving such medication (National Center for Health Statistics, 2011, Table 95). This trend is also evident internationally, as shown in Figure 3.2: for most OECD countries there was a doubling in the use of anti-depressant medication between 2000 and 2011. This may, of course, be attributable in part to the effectiveness of the pharmaceutical industry's marketing campaigns for these profitable products. However, the health effects of insecurity and stress are wider than that, as we explain in the next section.

Stress, work and health

One important body of research on the effects of stress on health has been conducted within workplaces. These studies have found that jobs with high psychological demands coupled with low levels of control were associated with increased exposure to stress and ill health. Psychological demands are such things as time pressure, high work pace, high workload and conflicting demands, while job control is defined as including control over workload, variety of work, and use and development of skills. This is known as the demand-control model (Karasek and Theorell, 1990; see Figure 3.3). Jobs characterized by high psychological demands in combination with low control are 'high stress' jobs because they do not enable individual autonomy and are often conducted in high pressure contexts. Work with high demands but also high control is termed 'active work', as the worker is able to manage his or her own workload and has a high degree of choice and autonomy over how the work is undertaken. Opportunities to learn new skills mitigate the stress-inducing effects of high strain in active jobs. Conversely, 'passive jobs', characterized by low demands and low control, are likely to

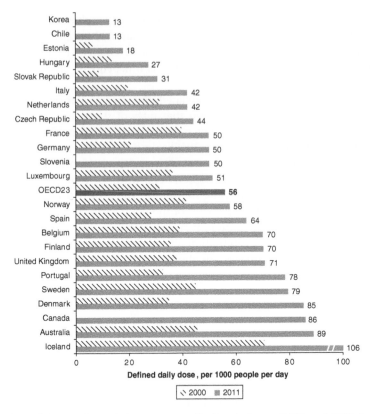

Figure 3.2 Rise in anti-depressant medication between 2000 and 2011 in the OECD countries
Source: OECD.

have fewer opportunities for learning. It has also been suggested that the presence of social support from co-workers and supervisors in the workplace might in some way moderate or act as a buffer to reduce ill-health effects (Johnson and Hall, 1988).

Workplace studies of the demand-control-support model have found that job control is an important determinant of health. High stress jobs lead to increased risk among employees of cardiovascular disease, including heart disease and stroke; increased risk of unhealthy behaviours, including poor diet, physical inactivity, heavy drinking and smoking; and obesity, musculoskeletal disorders such as back pain, and mental ill health, including depression, anxiety and emotional exhaustion (Bambra, 2011, pp. 81–87, 91–95). High stress jobs also

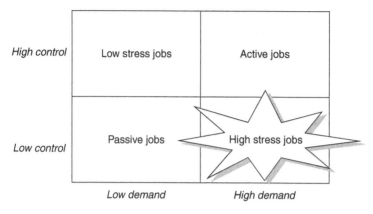

Figure 3.3 Visual representation of Karasek's model of job strain
Source: Adapted from Karasek and Theorell (1990).

contribute to health inequalities, as low job control accounted for approximately half of the social gradient in coronary heart disease in the Whitehall II study (Marmot et al., 1997; see Box 3.1).

Box 3.1 The Whitehall studies

The Whitehall studies, named for the street in London where much of the British civil service is located, are two large longitudinal studies of British civil servants set up to investigate (in the first instance) inequalities in coronary heart disease (CHD). Whitehall I, which began in 1967, followed 17,530 male civil servants; Whitehall II, which began in 1985 and at the time of writing (2014) is ongoing, is following 10,308 male and female civil servants. The original study decisively undercut the prevailing view that higher rates of CHD were experienced by high-status professionals and managers, and, in fact, found an 'inverse social gradient' in which risks for low-grade clerical workers were more than twice as high as for senior managers. Both Whitehall studies have subsequently identified similar inverse gradients across a broad range of adverse health outcomes. In other words, the person most likely to suffer adverse health effects is not the stereotypical hard-charging executive or ambitious professional, but, rather, the man

---

Box 3.1   (Continued)

or woman (and many such jobs are disproportionately held by women) working in a care home, serving food in a restaurant, cleaning or staffing a call centre – the kinds of jobs Ehrenreich and Toynbee found in their investigations, and on which millions of people now rely for survival. The Whitehall studies are also significant because serious material deprivation was almost certainly not an issue for most of the people studied; in other words, they make it possible to isolate the physiological effects of such psychosocial variables as position in a hierarchy. This said, they almost certainly understate the extent of the inverse socioeconomic gradient in health among the population as a whole: to assess this, we would need a study that included (in the case of London) not only civil servants but also building cleaners and fast food employees working on zero-hours contracts, and perhaps also investment bankers as well as civil servants.

A further set of stresses is associated with the spread of insecure employment. Job insecurity is associated with a number of adverse health outcomes, including worse rates of self-reported health, mental ill health and high blood pressure, as well as higher rates of smoking, drinking and unhealthy diet (Bambra, 2011, pp. 111–117). People in temporary employment also have higher mortality rates than those in secure employment, and poor-quality work with little security can be as damaging to health as unemployment (Benach and Muntaner, 2007). For example, one Australian study found that poor-quality jobs with low security, low marketability and high job strain were associated with poorer health when compared with work with few or no stressors (Broom et al., 2006). As suggested earlier, multiple mechanisms are probably at work here, and it is difficult to disentangle them.

Many workers on insecure contracts cycle from precarious work into unemployment – the 'low-pay, no-pay cycle' (Shildrick et al., 2012b) – thus augmenting the negative consequences for health. Working conditions have arguably become more stressful, and therefore more harmful to health, during this period of neoliberal ascendancy. Even before the financial crisis, workers in OECD countries reported substantial increases in working long hours and especially in work intensity between 1995 and 2006 (OCED, 2009, Annex 2).

Worklessness, unemployment and health

A second way in which neoliberal economic insecurity gets under our skin is via worklessness and unemployment. Worklessness refers to 'the unemployed' (defined as those out of work but looking for work), as well as those who have never worked and those who are deemed unable to work (e.g. due to ill health). The evolution of the term and its more frequent use within policy discourses, particularly in the UK, since the late 1990s reflects the emergence of neoliberalism in advanced economies and specifically the demise of full employment as a policy objective. In North America, 'unemployment' (usually defined with reference to official figures that may exclude a substantial number of the workless) is a more common term.

From the late 1940s until the mid-1970s, the advanced economies of the West experienced something close to full (male) employment, broadly understood as either official unemployment rates of less than 3 per cent or employment rates of over 80 per cent of the working-age population. There were, of course, periods of unemployment during the early post-war years, but these were cyclical, following the boom and bust of patterns of the economy (e.g. the early 1960s in the UK): in periods of economic growth there were jobs for all, while in periods of recession there was an increase in unemployment. To a large extent this cyclical pattern ended with the economic crisis of the 1970s and the subsequent rise of neoliberal economic models. The point here is simply that this overtly ideological policy change has led to the emergence of *structural* worklessness – long-term, permanent and non-cyclical lack of jobs – as a key characteristic of neoliberal economies.

At the same time, there was an expansion relative to the early post-war period in terms of those (e.g. women, lone parents) for whom work was expected, or required as an alternative to falling behind economically. At the time of writing, Elizabeth Warren is a US senator. Circa 2004, when still an academic, she pointed out that *all* the growth in median family income in the US between the 1970s and 2004 occurred because two-earner households had become the norm (Warren, 2007). Conversely, families with only one earner (including in particular those headed by single women) were falling behind, in relative terms. Meanwhile, as part of the neoliberal project to shrink the state (Chapter 1), neoliberalism has reduced the support provided to people when they are out of work – a level of support that varies widely among high-income countries (Scruggs and Allan, 2006); this variation underscores our emphasis on the importance of politics. For example, as an instance of the great risk shift, in the UK the percentage of an average production worker's wage that would be replaced by unemployment benefits (the unemployment replacement rate) for one earner supporting a partner and two children declined from 69 per cent in 1971 to 36 per cent in 1990, although increasing slightly under Labour governments post-1997. For a single worker with no dependents, the decline was more dramatic: from 54 per cent in 1971 to 20 per cent or less in every year post-1997 (Scruggs et al., 2014). These figures apply only to those workers who are eligible for benefits; a further issue involves eligibility for compensation, which varies widely among countries and, in some cases, has been one of the more conspicuous casualties of neoliberalism. In Canada, one of the more dramatic neoliberal retrenchments of social policy was a 1996 tightening of the eligibility criteria for the national program of unemployment insurance, such that 'the proportion of unemployed Canadians who actually receive[d] regular insurance benefits dropped dramatically, from 83 per cent of unemployed Canadians in 1980 to only 42 per cent in 1997' (Prince, 1999, p. 181).

Studies have consistently shown that unemployment increases the chances of poor health (Bambra and Eikemo, 2009). Empirical studies from the recessions of the 1980s and 1990s have shown that unemployment is associated with an increased likelihood of morbidity and mortality, including higher rates of poor mental health and suicide; all cause and specific causes of mortality; self-reported poor health and limiting long-term illness; and risky health behaviours, particularly problematic alcohol use and smoking (Bambra, 2011, pp. 102–111). As suggested by our earlier discussion, unemployment and precarious employment are also important causes of the within-country health inequalities that we discuss at greater length in Chapter 5.

A UK study found that recently unemployed young men were twice as likely to visit a GP for depression and anxiety as those in work (Montgomery et al., 1999a). Similarly, in terms of suicides, a study of young men in Scotland conducted in the 1980s found that the risk of suicide was double (Platt, 1986), while attempted suicide is ten times more likely in unemployed young men than in those in employment (Dorling, 2009). Other causes of death are also more common among the unemployed. For example, a study that examined the impact of loss of employment during the early 1980s recession on mortality among middle-aged British men found that the unemployed were twice as likely to die as those who remained in work (Morris et al., 1994). This included deaths from cardiovascular disease and cancers. The negative effects of unemployment on health are also evident in studies of self-reported health and long-term illnesses, with, for example, a study of UK men (Bartley and Plewis, 2002) finding that the unemployed were twice as likely to have a long-term health problem. Data also suggest that unemployment increases risky health behaviour. This is particularly the case among young men. For example, a study of British young men found that the unemployed were three times more likely to smoke or drink heavily than men who had never been unemployed (Montgomery et al., 1999b).

Unemployment is associated with poverty and social exclusion, and it tends to be concentrated among those with lower incomes, education or skills. The importance for health inequalities was demonstrated (Popham and Bambra, 2010) in an English study which found that more than 80 per cent of health differences between the most affluent and the least affluent people in the English workforce is due to unemployment: 6 per cent of men living in owner-occupied housing reported ill health compared with 19 per cent of men in social rented housing – a difference of 13 points. Once differences in employment status were taken into account, this difference reduced to three points, a reduction of over 80 per cent. Another study found that regional differences in unemployment – such as between the North and the South of England – also explained regional differences in levels of poor health (Moller et al., 2013).

Two pathways explain how unemployment results in poorer health: the material consequences of unemployment (income loss) and the psychosocial effects of unemployment (e.g. relative deprivation as a result of income loss, stigma, isolation and loss of self-worth). On the first point, especially over the longer term the unemployed suffer substantial income losses and the material consequences of unemployment. Around one in four unemployed men report feelings of shame related to unemployment (Bambra, 2011, p. 107), and an Italian study of factory workers who were made redundant found that their mental health got worse even though they were still given 100 per cent of their wages for the first six months of unemployment (Rudas et al., 1991). In the longer term, though, the unemployed suffer from a greatly reduced income, and many unemployed people live in relative poverty. In the UK, for example, against a background of rising prices for such essentials as food and transportation, circa 2013 out-of-work benefits for single adults covered only 38 per cent of the cost of a Minimum Income Standard developed by the Joseph Rowntree Foundation, and for households with children only 58 per cent (MacInnes et al., 2013, p. 24). For some of those out of work, in the UK and elsewhere, the consequences are even more grave, and are compounded by the cuts in other benefits described in Chapter 4.

Ill health itself is also a cause of worklessness. 'Health-related worklessness' is a term used to refer collectively to people who are out of work on a long-term basis (in the UK, over four weeks) due to a chronic illness or disability (Bambra, 2011, pp. 131–146). A disability in this context is defined as an illness or impairment that limits the usual activities of daily living, including work ability. Neoliberalism breeds vicious cycles. A study of trends in the UK (see Figures 3.5 and 3.6) has shown that the percentage of men reporting poor health has increased from 7 per cent of the working population in 1978 to 11 per cent in 2004, and for women this has increased from 11 per cent to 13 per cent. This was accompanied by a threefold increase in health-related worklessness, from 2 to 7 per cent for men and from 2 to 6 per cent for women during the same time period (Popham et al., 2012). This is hardly surprising, since poor health is a significant risk factor for job loss. For example, European and US studies have found that people who developed chronic health problems while in employment were twice as likely to become workless within a four-year period as those who remained healthy (McDonough and Amick, 2001; Schuring et al., 2009). In the US, where health insurance coverage, at least until recently, was closely tied to employment and even those with insurance often find it inadequate, a vicious cycle of special importance involves untreated illnesses related to loss of insurance coverage following job loss, creating a health poverty trap (frequently including personal bankruptcy) that can be extremely difficult to escape (Abelson, 2009; Dwyer, 2009; Himmelstein et al., 2009).

In most Western countries, long-term health-related worklessness carries an entitlement to receipt of financial support from the welfare state in the form of sickness and disability pensions or, in the case of the UK, incapacity-related benefits. Rates of receipt of these health-related benefits have increased over the last 30 years – and have become a feature of neoliberal structural worklessness. For example, in the UK the number of people who claim health-related benefits has increased from 0.5 million recipients in 1975 to 2.6 million in 2014 – around 7 per cent of the UK working-age population (Gabbay et al., 2011). Post-2010, the Conservative-led government in the UK initiated major and often dishonest efforts to reduce the cost of such benefits, which we discuss in more detail in Chapter 4. Across the Organisation for Economic Co-operation and Development (OECD) countries, around 6 per cent of the entire working-age population receive such benefits (OECD, 2009).

The most common causes of long-term sickness absence are mus-culoskeletal disorders (such as back pain), stress and mental health problems (especially depression and anxiety) (Bambra, 2011, p. 133). Internationally, mental health problems account for a third of new disability claims across OECD countries. Health-related worklessness contributes to health inequalities, as it varies by gender, education and region (Bambra, 2014):

- The employment rates of women (50 per cent) with a health condition or disability are lower in the UK than for men with similar levels of ill health (60 per cent).
- Health-related job losses are more likely among the least educated.
- There are substantial geographical inequalities in health-related worklessness, with rates highest in areas which have experienced rapid deindustrialization and the loss of manufacturing jobs.

Spatial variation in health-related worklessness is illustrated in Figure 3.4. This uses Standardized Illness Ratios, in which 100 represents the national average incapacity-related benefit recipient rate. Areas with values above 100 have of incapacity-related benefit receipt rates above the national average. These areas are depicted by dark grey and black shading. Areas with values below 100, shown by white and pale grey shading, have rates below the national average. Looking at data in this way shows that the receipt of incapacity-related benefits is concentrated in the de-industrialized areas of the North East of England and South Wales, as well as in former manufacturing centres such as Manchester and Liverpool. These areas are all shaded black, with receipt rates at least 50 per cent higher than the national average. Regional differences in worklessness rates contribute substantially to regional differences in health inequalities and to health inequalities between regions – as we discuss further in Chapter 5 (Bambra and Popham, 2010).

Health-related worklessness has emerged as a relatively new phe-nomenon over the 30-year period of neoliberal ascendancy (Chapter 1). There are debates as to whether this type of worklessness reflects a gen-uine increase in poorer health among certain social groups or whether it is a form of 'hidden unemployment' (Beatty and Fothergill, 2005; Bambra, 2011, pp. 145–150). In our view, there is evidence for both arguments, and, like many other candidate explanations for health inequalities, they are not mutually exclusive.

In terms of hidden unemployment (a term coined by Beatty and col-leagues, 2000), the rapid increase in health-related benefit claims across

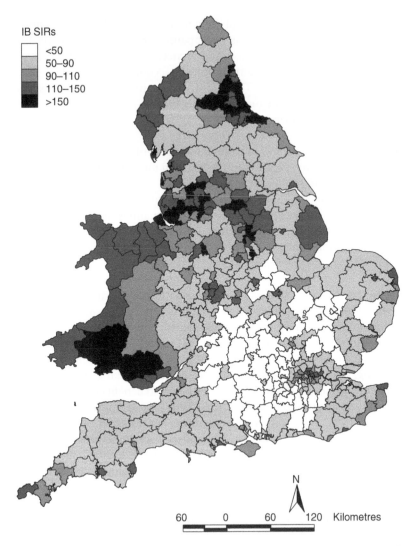

IB SIRs

☐ <50
50–90
90–110
110–150
■ >150

N

60   0   60   120 Kilometres

Figure 3.4 Standardized illness ratios of incapacity benefit claims by local authority, England and Wales

Source: Reproduced from Norman, P. and Bambra, C. (2007) 'The Utility of Medically Certified Sickness Absence as an Updatable Indicator of Population Health'. *Population, Space and Place*, *13*, 333–352, with permission from the publishers, John Wiley & Sons.

the OECD in the 1980s and 1990s coincided with similar decreases in the numbers in receipt of unemployment benefits (Figures 3.5 and 3.6), suggesting substitution between the two types of benefit schemes (OECD, 2009). This perception is also supported by the geographical distribution of health-related worklessness, which is skewed towards the de-industrialized areas. These areas lost thousands of jobs when their main industries, such as the coal, steel and shipping industries, were closed in the 1980s and 1990s, and, in the absence of a policy of full employment, there has not been sufficient replacement work in these localities. In the UK, Conservative governments also actively encouraged a transition to sickness benefits in these communities as a way of reducing the unemployment rate. By way of example, Beatty and colleagues (2007) estimate that the 'real' level of unemployment in the UK in 2007 was 2.6 million, compared with only 0.9 million claiming

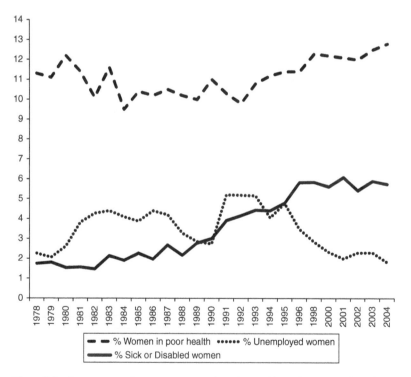

Figure 3.5 Percentage of women unemployed, workless due to ill health or disability or in poor health, UK, 1978–2004
Source: Data from Popham et al., 2012.

Figure 3.6   Percentage of men unemployed, workless due to ill health or disability or in poor health, UK, 1978–2004
Source: Data from Popham et al., 2012.

unemployment benefit (Jobseeker's Allowance), as they estimated that around 40 per cent of health-related benefit recipients would have been in work under full employment.

So, we argue that it is a case of both increased ill health (particularly mental ill health) *and* hidden unemployment leading to the explosion of health-related worklessness under neoliberalism as: (1) work-related ill health (particularly mental ill health) has increased as a damaging social by-product of neoliberal economic insecurity, the intensification of work and the epidemic of stress; and (2) the abandonment of full employment as part of the economic restructuring of neoliberalism and the subsequent rapid deindustrialization of certain regions has meant that for many areas there are simply no jobs to be had (hidden unemployment), which, in turn, can lead to an increase in ill health. This is a vicious cycle, one that is very much a feature of a neoliberal economics that puts profits before people and places.

Cross-national comparisons of the insecurity epidemic

Patterns in the distribution of stress, work insecurity and worklessness do not follow a universal international pattern. In this section, we draw on previous comparative work on national employment patterns, labour markets and social policies to provide a further basis for assessing the connections between neoliberalism and health. We show that in the most neoliberal countries stress has a worse effect on health than in those countries that are less neoliberal, while the health penalty of unemployment, and the unemployment penalty of ill health, is also higher in more neoliberal countries. This is because countries that have not been as much affected by the politics and economics of neoliberalism – largely the social democratic countries of northern Europe – have a more extensive regulatory state, which provides a better context within which to work as well as stronger support for those out of work. Stress and insecurity develop within a wider economic, political and social context.

First, the prevalence of stress is significantly higher in the most neoliberal countries and lower in the least, as the workplace is more regulated (particularly in Sweden or Norway). For example, a study of 12 European countries found that levels of workplace stress were higher in the more neoliberal UK (i.e. levels of low control at work were higher) than in the social democratic countries of Denmark and Sweden (Dragano et al., 2011).

Second, the effects on health of stressful work environments are also reduced in these countries, as, for example, workers with low job control in the UK were more than 2.5 times more likely to report depression, compared with only a 1.7 times higher likelihood in Denmark and Sweden (Dragano et al., 2011).

Third, the health effects of job insecurity or unemployment are also much less pronounced in the least neoliberal countries, as their more extensive social security systems improve the ability of individuals to cope with stressful events (Bartley and Blane, 1997). European research has shown that, while in all countries unemployed people report higher rates of poor health than those in employment, inequalities between the employed and the unemployed are largest in the most neoliberal countries (Bambra and Eikemo, 2009). For example, in 2011 the replacement value of out-of-work benefits in the UK for a single worker with no dependents was just 18 per cent and for a worker with dependents just 45 per cent, as compared with 60 per cent or higher for both categories in Sweden (Scruggs et al., 2014), and benefits were means tested and subject to strict criteria for eligibility assessment.[6] Fourth, less neoliberal countries, such as Finland, have smaller inequalities in stressful working conditions than more neoliberal countries, such as the UK, potentially resulting in smaller health inequalities among the workforce (Sekine et al., 2009).

Fifth, the onset of ill health is more likely to result in worklessness in more neoliberal countries. In Europe, health-related worklessness is lowest in the social democratic welfare states (an average of 38 per cent) and highest in the most neoliberal countries: in the UK 50 per cent and in Ireland 64 per cent of people with a health problem are workless. Continental European countries have an average worklessness rate of 48 per cent, while in southern Europe it is around 52 per cent (van der Wel et al., 2012). In all countries, worklessness rates are particularly high among people who have both a health problem and low education. However, the study found that the employment rates of those with a health problem and low education are higher in countries that invest in active labour market policies, have higher levels of income equality and provide more generous welfare benefits (van der Wel et al., 2012).

Like the comparisons of labour market policy cited earlier, these observations underscore the importance of political choices. In the aftermath of the financial crisis that began in 2008, a variety of protections against the health consequences of insecurity are under renewed attack in the name of austerity and deficit reduction. The nature of that attack, its ideological connections with neoliberalism and the consequences for health are the topic of the next chapter.

4
Austerity: How Politics Has Pulled Away Our Safety Net

David Stuckler and Sanjay Basu (2013) introduce their book on austerity and its health consequences with the case of a stroke-paralysed man with limited ability to walk who was cut off disability benefits by Atos Healthcare, a corporation given a contract by the Conservative-led UK government to cut its benefit costs by (re)assessing applicants, with abundant subsequent evidence of inadequate performance that eventually led to the end of the contract (Ramesh, 2013; Wintour, 2013; Butler, 2014a; Syal, 2014). This example captures three dimensions of the neoliberal turn in social policy: the perceived imperative of cutting costs; the presumption of undeservingness applied to benefit claimants, in contrast to the corporate recipients of public subsidies; and the privatization of core public service functions that have serious consequences for the daily lives of their clients (Seabrook, 2013). Here we first describe the origins of the crisis in neoliberal policies of deregulation that left financial markets to 'do their thing', and then examine the impacts and politics of the austerity programs that have represented the neoliberal response to the crisis. We end the chapter with a provocative comparison with development policies that advanced neoliberalism outside the high-income world.

The financial crisis of 2008: The opportunity for the austerity epidemic

The basic facts about the financial crisis that spread across the world in 2008 are now familiar. The policies that made it possible, and perhaps inevitable, began decades earlier, but the sequence of events began in 2007, as investors became concerned about the quality of the high-risk or subprime mortgages that had been packaged ('securitized') and sold on financial markets, and the market for these securities quickly collapsed. Despite efforts by the US Federal Reserve to contain the crisis, its effects quickly spread through the highly leveraged US financial sector[7] and to other high-income countries, revealing what the Bank of England described with masterful understatement as 'under-appreciated, but potent, interconnections between firms in the global financial system' (Bank of England, 2008, p. 9).[8] Among the more visible milestones in 2008 were the failure of the investment bank Bear Stearns and the bankruptcy of Lehman Brothers in the US and the temporary nationalization of Northern Rock in the UK. In short order, governments – again, mainly in the US and the UK – offered an estimated US$14 trillion in cash and credit guarantees to rescue financial institutions (Bank of England, 2009). Even this initiative could not avoid a contraction of credit that led to a recession deeper than any downturn since the Great Depression, and, at least in the UK, longer (Clark and Heath, 2014, p. 15). Officially reported levels of unemployment roughly doubled from pre-crisis levels to maximum levels of 10.6 per cent in the US and 8.5 per cent in the UK. The figures are not directly comparable; more importantly – as suggested in the previous chapter – there are reasons to consider them a serious underestimate of real-world economic impacts. For example, at the epicentre of the crisis in the US, adding to official figures the number of people who had given up looking for work ('discouraged workers') and those in part-time work because that was all that was available generated a total unemployment rate of 18 per cent rather than 10.6 per cent in January 2010 (Bureau of Labor Statistics, 2011). Again in the US, the number of low-income people receiving food stamps rose from 26.6 million in July 2007 to 41.8 million in July 2010 and to more than 47 million, or roughly one in seven Americans, in later years, with millions more eligible (Food Research and Action Center, various years). Between early 2009 and late 2010, more than 300,000 American households lost their homes every month in foreclosures (repossessions, in British terminology), up from approximately 75,000 circa 2005 (RealtyTrac, 2014). The effect was to create a largely invisible cohort of several million dispossessed households, many of them renters who were evicted after property owners defaulted (Sassen, 2011).

These were the first impacts of the crisis. The second set resulted from a combination of reduced government tax revenues, as incomes and profits shrank, and heavy borrowing to finance stimulus spending and the rising cost of social protection based on pre-crisis benefit levels. In other words, the financial crisis led to a fiscal crisis for national governments – a problem that was especially severe in countries such as Ireland and Spain, where debt-financed property bubbles collapsed just as they had somewhat earlier in the US. Predictably, government debt as a percentage of gross domestic product (GDP) rose across the high-income world, as it had in the wake of previous financial crises. This, in turn, led to a further problem, concentrated in Europe: the investors and credit rating agencies whose judgements constitute the verdict of 'financial markets' became concerned that some countries – initially Greece, where government debt had risen to approximately 200 per cent of GDP by 2013, but also other countries such as Ireland and Portugal – would be unable to pay back the debt, creating a risk of default. Consequently, the interest rate demanded by investors before they would buy bonds issued by these countries – the risk premium – increased dramatically, as, therefore, did those governments' cost of borrowing (Scharpf, 2013).

This concern about default risk, and actual or anticipated rises in borrowing costs, was the immediate justification for the third set of crisis impacts: the drastic but selective public expenditure cuts that are a central focus of this chapter, now conventionally labelled as austerity. In addition to their direct impacts, austerity programs have had the effect of reducing domestic demand for goods and services, often worsening the initial downturn. The result was disastrous levels of officially reported unemployment in the worst-hit countries: 14 per cent in Ireland, the former Celtic Tiger, and more than 20 per cent in Spain and Greece (more than 50 per cent among people under 25). Across the entire Eurozone, unemployment among those under 25 had risen to almost one in four by late 2013 (Inman, 2013). As we show in the next chapter, the distribution of unemployment and its consequences varied according to a number of characteristics other than age, thus contributing to the ratcheting up of inequality. However, austerity was not confined to Eurozone countries considered to be at high risk of default. Some of the most draconian austerity measures were promoted in the UK, which was never considered a default risk and where government debt as a percentage of GDP, although it increased as an inevitable consequence of recession, was only slightly higher than Germany's and lower than that of the US. This is an oversimplification, since the actual ratio of debt to GDP is only one indicator of creditworthiness, but it suffices to make the point.

Before we explore the politics of austerity and its consequences for health, it is important to understand the financial crisis itself as a consequence or legacy of neoliberal policy choices, in particular the deregulation of financial markets and institutions and an obliteration of distinctions between corporate and public interests. As noted in the preceding chapter, the Reagan and Thatcher governments increased interest rates in order to reduce inflation, accepting the collateral damage of increased unemployment. Simultaneously, the US in particular was deregulating its domestic financial industry, at the well-financed behest of the industry itself and – in the Reagan era – under a secretary of the treasury who was a former CEO of the brokerage firm Merrill Lynch (Johnson and Kwak, 2011, pp. 70–87; Krippner, 2011, pp. 86–105). The presumption appeared to be that markets could do no wrong, and deregulation contributed to a pattern of 'financialization' in which a rising percentage of the profits of US corporations, on a variety of measures, came from finance rather than from producing goods or directly providing services (Krippner, 2011, pp. 27–57). Some of these profits were achieved by corporate restructurings that shed jobs while maximizing shareholder value over the short term, as we noted in the preceding chapter. Additionally, the subprime mortgages that, once securitized and sold on, triggered the crisis are best understood by analogy with corporate strategies for increasing profits by reducing labour costs. As sociologist Saskia Sassen points out, 'with these instruments, housing becomes an efficient mechanism for getting at the savings of households worldwide – a form of primitive accumulation that moves faster than extracting profit from lowering wages' (Sassen, 2009, p. 412; see also Newman, 2009).

In the UK, financial deregulation was driven by the desire to compete with the US (in the first instance, New York) as a global financial centre (Helleiner, 1994), and by the preference (noted earlier) for finance rather than production as a driver of growth. The extent to which this had become conventional wisdom across the British political spectrum in the years before the crisis can be gauged from a famous 2004 speech by Gordon Brown (then Labour finance minister, later prime minister), in which he noted London's pre-eminence as a global financial centre and emphasized that further financial deregulation and other measures to 'encourage the risk takers' would be part of the government's future agenda (Brown, 2004). Obliviousness to any distinction between public and corporate interests would continue into the crisis itself, especially in the US, where the response was led by Treasury Secretary Henry Paulson, a former CEO of the investment bank Goldman Sachs.

Another useful analogy involves the microeconomic concept of negative externalities, exemplified by pollution emitted by factories or mines that kills farmers' crops or leads to respiratory disease among people living downwind. To the extent that no institutions exist to require compensation for the damage done – that is, to 'internalize' the costs – the factory or mine owners are profiting from damaging the lives and livelihoods of others. The damage done by the financial crisis, along with publicly financed bailouts of financial institutions that had been allowed to become too big to fail, represents the externalized or socialized cost of accumulating private fortunes in the financial services industry – a manifestation of the great risk shift in which the ultra-rich shifted their risk to the public as a whole, as its services were cut back and its future incomes borrowed against. And the bargaining power the industry acquired as individual institutions became too big to fail enabled it to engage in what was described early in the course of the crisis as a hostage-taking (Lordon, 2008), with national economies and the livelihoods of millions of people as the hostages.

Austerity politics and the ideological creation of an epidemic

Nothing is new about retrenchment in spending on social protection (a term we prefer to welfare), although most European countries embarked on this course later than their North American counterparts. In Canada and the US, the turning points were (respectively) the 1995 national government budget, which incorporated many measures that had been recommended in a confidential report by the International Monetary Fund's 1994 mission to Canada (obtained by Halifax Initiative, 1999), and the 'welfare reform' legislation signed into law by President Clinton in 1996. This legislation ended a decades-old federal guarantee of minimal financial assistance to families with children (Aid to Families with Dependent Children, or AFDC), replacing it with a time-limited package of assistance conditional on active efforts to find work of any kind ('workfare'), even for mothers with very young children. By 1995, the real median value of AFDC payments for a family of four had already been reduced to just half its value in 1970 (Wacquant, 2009, p. 49). The legislation delivered on a campaign pledge to 'end welfare as we know it', in a climate of toxic, racially tinged rhetoric about 'dependency' (Fraser and Gordon, 1994) and against a background in which polemicist Charles Murray had raised alarms for a decade about the dangers of a growing (workless, feckless and promiscuous) underclass. Murray claimed that the availability of welfare created incentives for the expansion of such a class, but he was at least as concerned with containing it: recognizing (in his view) that the best the US economy could offer many people was 'probably no more than getting by'; that '[t]o promise much more is a fraud'; and that consent from the new economy's losers must be enforced through 'negative incentives' – prison or a level of economic hardship 'so uncomfortable that any job will be preferable to' an existence on welfare (Murray, 1984, pp. 176–177).

The title of the welfare reform legislation was revealing, if Orwellian: the *Personal Responsibility* and *Work Opportunity* Reconciliation Act[9] – language incorporating the neoliberal propositions that the primary responsibility for economic success or failure rests with individuals, and that work opportunities are, in fact, available (despite the US labour market's long-standing failure to provide full employment). Welfare reform resulted in a rapid reduction in the income support rolls, although this may have been partly a result of bureaucratic stratagems (Ridzi and London, 2006), and was therefore judged a success over the short term. Some of its worst impacts were blunted for a while by the economic growth of the late 1990s, but, even so, a decade on, many families that had left welfare for work were living in poverty, trapped in low-wage jobs and facing problems with access to health care and child care that the legislation had done nothing to address (Schleiter and Statham, 2002; Seccombe, 2009). The 'reforms' must, therefore, be understood in part as a labour market policy that expanded the pool of low-wage labour, with some evidence suggesting that this contributed to political support for the changes (Websdale, 2001, p. 71; Wacquant, 2009, pp. 87, 93–98).

On the other side of the Atlantic, what might be thought of as a kinder, gentler variant of the neoliberal approach to social provision was unfolding under the rubric of the social investment state. Against a background of Thatcher-era privatizations, deindustrialization and labour market deregulation, Anthony Giddens argued that the welfare state needed to be replaced by a 'social investment state' in which the paradigm for access to livelihood is business formation rather than salaried employment, and in which it is necessary 'to shift the relationship between risk and security involved in the welfare state, to develop a society of "responsible risk takers" in the spheres of government, business enterprise and labour markets' (Giddens, 1998, pp. 100, 117). Jenson and Saint-Martin (2003) emphasize the social investment perspective's congruence with neoliberalism: 'In this discourse, it is acceptable for the state to spend generously when, and only when, it is behaving like a good business would, seeking to increase the promise of *future* profits' (p. 83; emphasis in original). Many of the social policies of the Labour government between 1997 and 2010, in particular the emphasis on investing in children, reflected elements of the social investment perspective (Dobrowolsky, 2002). Outside the high-income world, homologous developments were manifested in a World Bank strategy document, *From Safety Net to Springboard*, that redefined social policy's fundamental task as social risk management (Holzmann and Jörgensen, 2001), based on the initial presumption that 'In an ideal world with perfectly symmetrical information and complete, well-functioning markets, all risk management arrangements can and should be market-based (except for the incapacitated)' (p. 16). Thus, if governmental intervention to help the non-incapacitated poor is justified, this is only because of market failures resulting from the fact that the poor 'are more vulnerable than other population groups because they are typically more exposed to risk and have little access to appropriate risk management instruments' (p. 10). Here, again, we see the great risk shift at work, with responsibility privatized and individualized.

We cannot provide a detailed history of the political and ideological antecedents of today's austerity prescriptions. This brief summary suffices to show the context that neoliberalism has provided for responses to the financial crisis of 2008. Even some progressive academics, such as Schäfer and Streeck (2013) and most of the authors in their book on *Politics in the Age of Austerity*, argue that the combination of recession and the cumulative build-up of government debt over the preceding decades leaves governments little room for manoeuvre for any expansion of social protection. Whether or not one accepts this rather bleak prognosis, to which we return in Chapter 6, the more immediate point is one made by contributors to the *Age of Austerity* volume, with which there can be little disagreement:

> If one considers the decade before 2008 as the trial run for a new wave of even more incisive consolidation of public finances in rich democracies ... one cannot but arrive at dire predictions concerning the future capacities of governments to assist their societies in coping with changed conditions of prosperity and equality.
>
> (Streeck and Mertens, 2013, p. 55)

It may be helpful to borrow terminology from the software industry, in which successive versions of a program build on the basic architecture of preceding releases while adding functions and relying on a certain level of user familiarity. If labour market transformations that began in the 1970s represent neoliberalism 1.0, and the uneven social policy retrenchments of the pre-crisis era represent neoliberalism 2.0, what we are now experiencing is the rollout of neoliberalism 3.0 (beta version).

We return in Chapter 6 to questions of political possibility: whether the software can be returned to the publisher for a refund, and replaced by a product with less destructive human impacts than those described in the material that follows.

The contours of the austerity epidemic

In Greece, Spain, Portugal and Ireland, some of the most immediate effects of austerity were observed in cuts to budgets for the public financing of health care, leading to increases in user charges for health services and prescription drugs (Karanikolos et al., 2013; Burke et al., 2014), while wage cuts and rising unemployment were making these charges more difficult to pay for those affected. In the UK – more specifically England, which is our focus in this section of the chapter – the pattern was somewhat different. Although since a Conservative-led government came to power a shift towards privatization of the National Health Service (NHS) has occurred, and is described in the next chapter, the major manifestation of (selective) austerity has involved substantial cuts in social protection under the rubric of welfare reform (see Hamnett, 2014) and local government budgets. In 2010, Conservative Prime Minister David Cameron famously declared that 'we are all in it together', but the actual record of spending cuts shows that nothing could be further from the truth. The impacts are falling disproportionately on the poorest and most vulnerable, while others continue to be insulated from the impacts of crisis and even to continue receiving public subventions of various kinds.

Table 4.1 lists the main austerity-driven 'reforms' to social protection since 2010 – changes that will not only reduce the incomes of benefit claimants, but also significantly widen the gaps in prosperity between the best and worst local economies across the UK (Beatty and Fothergill, 2014). It is estimated that, by the time currently planned welfare reforms have come into full effect in 2017, they will take nearly £19 billion a year out of the economy, primarily out of the pockets of people at the bottom of the income scale. This is equivalent to around £470 a year for every adult of working age in the country. The biggest losses arise from reforms to incapacity benefits (£4.3 billion a year), changes to tax credits (£3.6 billion a year) and capping the annual up-rating of most working-age benefits to only 1 per cent – well below inflation (£3.4 billion a year). The housing benefit reforms, reducing payments to claimants who are living in accommodation with an 'extra' bedroom, result in more modest losses – an estimated £490 million a year arising

Table 4.1 Summary of welfare reforms since 2010

Date	Measure
January 2011	Child trust fund abolished
April 2011	Child benefit frozen until 2015
April 2012	A one-year time limit to the receipt of contributory employment support allowance (ESA) for people in the work-related activity group
	Tax credits withdrawn from 'middle income' families
May 2012	Lone parent obligations introduced
October 2012	Conditionality, sanctions and hardship payments introduced
January 2013	Child benefit withdrawn from individuals earning more than £50,000
March 2013	Housing benefit/local housing allowance restricted to the consumer prices index – as are other benefits
April 2013	Child care costs covered by working tax credit cut from 80 per cent to 70 per cent
	Council tax benefit – 10 per cent reduction for welfare recipients in total payments to local authorities
	Up-rating of working-age benefits not related to disability restricted to 1 per cent (inflation 3.5 per cent)
	Household benefit cap (£500 per week for couple and lone parent households and £350 per week for single households)
	Social fund replaced by locally determined schemes for crisis loans and community care grants
	Under-occupancy charge or 'bedroom tax' if claimant has one spare bedroom (14 per cent reduction) or more (25 per cent reduction)
	Restrictions in access to legal aid
From April 2013	Migration of all existing working-age disability living allowance (DLA) claimants onto personal independence payment (PIP)
June 2013	Replacement of disability living allowance (DLA) by personal independence payment (PIP) for all new claims
October 2013	Universal credit pilots – new system of in- and out-of-work benefits with additional work-related activity requirements for claimants
December 2013	PIP reassessment of DLA claims
February 2015	Universal credit – planned national rollout

Source: Bambra and Garthwaite (2014); for a description of the major categories of welfare expenditure in Britain see Hamnett (2014).

from the under-occupancy charge (most commonly referred to as the 'bedroom tax') – but for the households affected the sums are, nevertheless, still large and destructive and can result in significant hardship (Butler, 2014b).

An analysis released late in 2014 made two fundamental points about the austerity program. First, Britons were clearly not 'all in it together' (De Agostini et al., 2014). Cuts between 2010 and 2014/2015 resulted in losses to people in the bottom half of the income distribution, with the poorest groups (those already facing the hardest times) losing most as a percentage of their incomes, while most people in the top half, with the exception of a few at the very top, saw increases in their incomes. Changes planned for the post-2015 period were anticipated to intensify the losses, in particular (and with a few exceptions) of people in the bottom half of the income distribution and of lone parents and large families. Second, the net effect of the changes 'was *neutral* overall, rather than contributing to deficit reductions' because of tax reductions (De Agostini et al., 2014, p. 5). This is consistent with the hypothesis that the imperative of deficit reduction is, in fact, a sham, a pretext for policies of redistributing income upward and risk downward.

In spatial terms, the financial impact of the reforms varies greatly across the country, with the economies of those local authorities with the highest prevalence of economic deprivation losing the most per working-age adult (Beatty and Fothergill, 2014). Older industrial areas, a number of seaside towns and some low-income London boroughs, which derive few beneficial spinoffs from nearby concentrations of almost unimaginable wealth, are hit hardest. The worst-hit local authority areas lose around four times as much, per adult of working age, as the authorities least affected by the reforms – affluent areas in the South and East of England outside London. Blackpool, in North West England, is hit worst of all – an estimated loss to the local economy of more than £900 a year for every working-age adult. More than two-thirds of the 50 local authority districts worst affected by the reforms could be described as older industrial areas, already hard-hit by the effects of deindustrialization and the collapse of mining (Hamnett, 2014). Even *The Economist* has described the impact as brutal ('City sicker', 2013).

The impact of these cuts is compounded by cuts to local government budgets. Subventions from central government make up a substantial part of local government budgets, and these governments are severely limited in their taxing powers and ability to raise revenues from other sources. An analysis by an alliance of local governments outside London found that governments in England's poorest regions would face the largest budget cuts, while London and the affluent South East would

£ per head.

- £0–£100
- £100–£150
- £150–£200
- >£200

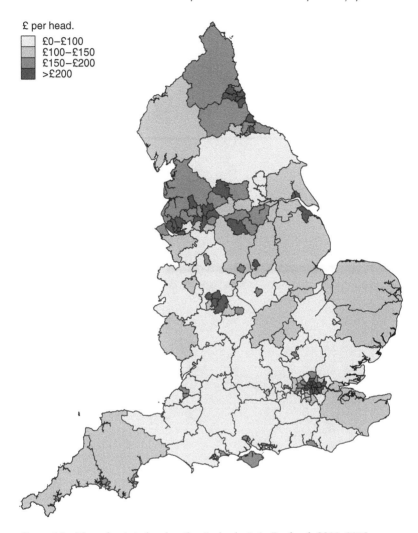

Figure 4.1 Map of cuts to local authority budgets in England, 2010–2015

Source: Reproduced with the permission of the Centre for Local Economic Strategies from M. Whitehead (Chair), C. Bambra, B. Barr et al., *Due North: Report of the Inquiry on Health Equity for the North* (Liverpool and Manchester: University of Liverpool and Centre for Local Economic Strategies, 2014). Map produced by Ben Barr, University of Liverpool, using data from Department for Communities and Local Government, *Local Government Financial Settlement*.

actually see increases (Special Interest Group, 2013). Figures 4.1 and 4.2 show the impacts of selective austerity by local authority area. A further dimension involves cuts in public employment, which is distributed unevenly across the country. Pearce (2013, p. 2034) points out that

£ per working age
adult per year.

☐ £0–£200
▨ £200–£300
▨ £300–£500
■ >£500

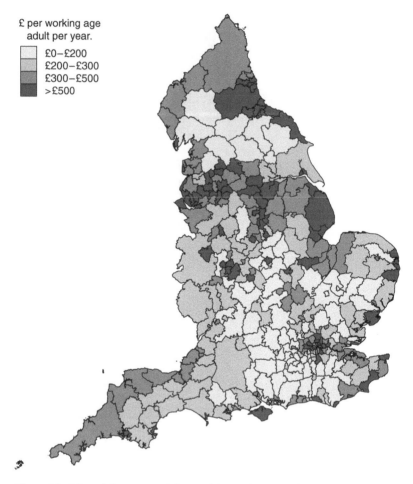

Figure 4.2   Map of the projected financial losses due to welfare reform by English local authority, 2010–2015

Source: Reproduced with the permission of the Centre for Local Economic Strategies from M. Whitehead (Chair), C. Bambra, B. Barr et al., *Due North: Report of the Inquiry on Health Equity for the North* (Liverpool and Manchester: University of Liverpool and Centre for Local Economic Strategies, 2014). Map produced by Ben Barr, University of Liverpool, using data from Beatty, C. and Fothergill, S. (2013) *Hitting the Poorest Places Hardest: The Local and Regional Impact of Welfare Reform* (Sheffield: Centre for Regional Economic and Social Research, Sheffield Hallam University).

public employment as a proportion of total employment ranges from 28.3 per cent in Northern Ireland to 16.5 per cent in South East England. Further, between 2008 and 2012 London actually experienced a small increase in public sector employment, while it declined by 12 per cent in the relatively poor North East. Some of the regions where these cumulative impacts will fall most heavily are already poorer than any regions in France, Germany, Belgium, the Netherlands, Luxembourg, Austria, Ireland, Denmark, Finland and Sweden (Eurostat, 2014).

This point becomes clearer when we consider effects on poverty, defined in this context as a household income below 60 per cent of the median household income. Poverty rates have risen substantially during austerity, with rates at the highest level in 30 years according to the largest study of poverty and deprivation ever conducted in the UK (Poverty and Social Exclusion, 2014a). The regions with the lowest levels of poverty were the South East (17 per cent) and the East (18 per cent). Rates were much higher in the northern regions, with 22 per cent in the North East, 23 per cent in the North West and 24 per cent in Yorkshire and Humber. The region with the highest level of poverty is London (28 per cent) (MacInnes et al., 2013), even as the capital also features concentrations of stratospheric wealth. Child poverty has also increased substantially, with 3.5 million children (more than one in four) now living in poverty in the UK. Child poverty was reduced dramatically between 1998 and 2012, when 1.1 million children were lifted out of poverty. Post-crisis austerity threatens to undo that progress, with an expected 600,000 more children living in poverty by 2015/2016 and 1.2 million more, to a total of 4.7 million, by 2020 (Child Poverty Action Group, 2014).

As a result of a combination of falling wages, rising prices and the erosion of social protection (Ashton et al., 2014; Cooper et al., 2014), emergency food banks, already well established as a feature of the social policy landscape in countries such as Canada (Tarasuk et al., 2014), have become an increasingly prominent symbol of the impoverishing effects of austerity in the UK (O'Dowd, 2013; Taylor-Robinson et al., 2013). The Trussell Trust, a Christian social action charity that is the largest operator of emergency food banks (and provides only three days' worth of food aid at a time), alone distributed 900,000 parcels in 2013–2014, up from 41,000 in 2009, and it has been estimated that 500,000 people relied on some form of food aid (Lambie-Mumford and Dowler, 2014). Throughout the UK, Trussell Trust figures from the first four months of 2014 show that benefit delays and changes accounted for 46 per cent of referrals. Interviews with food bank users confirmed the importance of waits for benefits, problems with disability benefits and tax credits and sanctions – when payments are temporarily stopped as a consequence of claimants' failure or inability to comply with work-seeking requirements (Perry et al., 2014); the interviews indicate that incorrect application of official criteria and failure to inform benefit claimants of all their options often play a role. 'It's actually destroying people's lives because they don't realise that £26 is a lot of money in this situation', said one interviewee about the application of the housing under-occupancy charge (the bedroom tax).

Alongside food poverty, many are also experiencing fuel poverty as energy costs rise. A household is defined as being in fuel poverty if it needs to spend more than 10 per cent of its income on fuel to maintain a satisfactory heating regime. In 2011, the number of fuel-poor households in England was estimated at around 2.39 million, representing approximately 11 per cent of all English households (Department of Energy and Climate Change, 2013). The poorest tenth of households spent *more than a fifth* of their budget on fuel, and the number of UK children living in fuel poverty had risen to 1.6 million – 130,000 more than in 2010 (Levell and Oldfield, 2011). A more recent estimate, perhaps reflecting the impact of subsequent benefit cuts, was that 'one in three people cannot afford to heat their homes adequately in the winter' (Poverty and Social Exclusion, 2014b). Fuel poverty is one of the influences pushing people living on low incomes to take out payday loans at extortionate interest rates to pay for basic necessities, or to resort to theft (Butler, 2013a, 2013b).

When asked to describe how 'the benefit changes will affect the health of people in my house', 75 per cent of all respondents in a series of studies by the Northern Housing Consortium (2014a) felt that welfare reform was having a negative impact on their health and well-being, as the following quotation illustrates:

> My husband's mental health never improves because his life is horrible. We exist day to day, we don't have anything to look forward to. We cannot get out of the situation we are in because we are too ill to work to improve our income.
>
> (Northern Housing Consortium, 2014b, p. 19)

It is against this background that we should consider Britain's effort to cut benefit costs by reducing sickness benefits and requiring fitness-for-work assessments. Garthwaite (2014) found that the stress associated with anticipating such assessments was itself destructive, an impact compounded not only by the poverty and insecurity associated with life on benefits but also stigmatization of benefit recipients as 'scroungers' and 'benefit cheats' – rhetoric that is increasingly common in the media (Garthwaite, 2011). Garthwaite's research (2014, p. 784) further emphasizes the perversity of the neoliberal 'presumption that work – any work – is a positive outcome for the individual as a good citizen and for society', a presumption that 'ignores the reality of precarious work characterized by insecurity, such as zero hours contracts and temporary agency work'. These forms of work organization are, as we saw in Chapter 3, increasingly common.

The health impacts of economic downturns and the austerity epidemic

Overall, the evidence clearly suggests that major economic downturns have detrimental effects. Perhaps the most dramatic case in recent history is the implosion of the Russian economy after the collapse of the Soviet Union, involving a reduction in economic output of roughly 50 per cent, massive capital flight, official poverty levels of 40 per cent, the disintegration of health care and social provision and a decline of several years in male life expectancy (Field, 2000; Field et al., 2000; Shkolnikov et al., 2004; Leon et al., 2009). The most drastic increases were in deaths from violence, cardiovascular disease and liver disease, proximally related to a drastic increase in alcohol consumption. However, alcohol consumption is far from the entire story, as it cannot explain increases in undernutrition, diphtheria and tuberculosis, and should itself be treated as a consequence of economic implosion and social disintegration. Further, the stresses associated with these processes are likely to have had a substantial and independent effect on health (Marmot and Bobak, 2000). A similar point about social disintegration can be made about mortality from chronic liver disease in Scotland, which rose starting circa 1975, and more rapidly after 1990, from among the lowest age-standardized rates in Europe to the highest by 2000, against a background of deindustrialization and social disorganization in western and central Scotland, in particular (Walsh et al., 2010; Whyte and Ajetunmobi, 2012).

In less dramatic situations, the epidemiological literature suggests that the short-term population health effects of recessions are mixed (Bambra, 2011, pp. 105–108), with the majority of international studies concluding that all-cause mortality, deaths from cardiovascular disease, motor vehicle accidents and hazardous health behaviours *decrease* during economic downturns. Notably, road traffic accidents decrease during periods of recession, as people have less need to drive, and are less able to afford to (Bambra, 2011). Conversely, deaths from suicides, rates of mental ill health and chronic illnesses *increase* in some – but not all – countries (Stuckler and Basu, 2013). A number of studies have found that health – particularly mental health – deteriorates during periods of recession. For instance, stress and depression were found to increase during periods of recession in studies in England, Spain, Greece and Northern Ireland, in some cases resulting in an increase in suicide (Bambra et al, in press). Perhaps most importantly, both unemployment and precarious employment increase during recessions, and they are strongly associated with a variety of adverse health outcomes, as noted in Chapter 3.

Substantial variations across countries have been found in the effects of recessions and economic downturns on population health. Stuckler and Basu (2013) found that the population health effects of recessions vary significantly by political and policy context, with those countries (such as Iceland and the US) that responded to the financial crisis of 2007 with an economic stimulus faring better, particularly in terms of mental health and suicides, than those countries (e.g. Spain, Greece and the UK) that chose to pursue a policy of austerity (public expenditure cuts to reduce government debt). Similarly, Hopkins (2006) found that in Thailand and Indonesia, where social welfare spending decreased during the Asian recession of the late 1990s, mortality rates increased. However, in Malaysia, where no cut-backs occurred, mortality rates were unchanged. Similarly, a study of European countries concluded that greater spending on social welfare could considerably reduce suicide rates during periods of economic downturn (Stuckler and Basu, 2013).

The health effects of recessions are unequally distributed across the population, thereby exacerbating health inequalities – again with some variation by country/political context (Bambra et al., in press). For example, a study of the Japanese working-age population found that economic downturn increased inequalities in self-rated health among men (Kondo et al., 2008), while a Finnish study found that the economic downturn slowed down the trend towards increased inequalities in mortality (Valkonen et al., 2000). A comparative study of self-reported health found that there was a more negative impact on the health of the most vulnerable in England than in Sweden during recessions (Copeland et al., 2015). The health effects of recessions may well, therefore, be experienced quite differently by otherwise similar individuals and communities due to national policy variation, with more generous welfare systems protecting the health of the population and especially the most vulnerable (Bambra et al., in press). This may be because comparatively strong social safety nets provide a buffer against the structural pressures towards widening health inequalities. The welfare states of the social democratic countries (described in Chapter 1) – in contrast to others – seem to *protect* the health of the most vulnerable during economic downturns. That health impacts of recession can be either ameliorated or magnified by public policy is the central message of Stuckler and Basu (2013). The historical record suggests that cutting welfare state entitlements leads to increased health inequalities – that is, lost years of health and life for the most vulnerable while the rest of us carry on in relative comfort. In this vein, Pearce (2013) points out that, even in cases where the overall health effect of recession across the entire population is minimal over the short term, such population averages – as in other cases – may conceal substantial inequalities in impact, defined by class and/or geography. For example, a US study found that, while premature mortality (deaths under age 75) and infant mortality rates (deaths before age 1) declined overall in all income quintiles from 1960 to 2002, inequalities by income and ethnicity decreased only between 1966 and 1980, and then increased between 1980 and 2002 (Krieger et al., 2008). The reductions in inequalities (1966–1980) occurred during a period of welfare expansion in the US (the 'War on Poverty') and the enactment of civil rights legislation which increased access to health care and welfare state services. The increases in health inequalities occurred during the Reagan–Bush period of welfare state retrenchment, when public welfare services (including health care insurance coverage) were cut, funding of social assistance was reduced, the minimum wage was frozen and the tax base was shifted from the rich to the poor, leading to increased income polarization. These findings are replicated in studies of welfare state restrictions in New Zealand (Shaw et al., 2005; Blakely et al., 2008), which found that, while general mortality rates declined, inequalities among men, women and children in all-cause mortality increased in the 1980s and the 1990s, then stabilized in the early 2000s. The increases occurred during a period in which New Zealand underwent major structural reform (including a less redistributive tax system, targeted social benefits, regressive tax on consumption introduced, privatization of major utilities and public housing, user charges for welfare services and a more deregulated labour market). Conversely, the stabilization of inequalities in mortality in the late 1990s and early 2000s occurred during a period in which the economy improved and there were some improvements in services (e.g. better access to social housing, more generous social assistance and a decrease in health care costs). Research into the health effects of Thatcherism (1979–1990) has also concluded that neoliberalism, the large scale dismantling of the

UK's social democratic institutions and the early pursuit of austerity-style policies increased health inequalities. Thatcherism deregulated the labour and financial markets, privatized utilities and state enterprises, restricted social housing, curtailed trade union rights, marketized the public sector, significantly cut the social wage via welfare state retrenchment, accepted mass unemployment and implemented large tax cuts for the business sector and the most affluent (Scott-Samuel et al., 2014). In this period, while life expectancy increased and mortality rates decreased for all social groups, the increases were greater and more rapid among the highest social groups, so that inequalities increased. These rises were not inevitable: in the UK – as in the US and New Zealand – inequalities in mortality declined from the 1920s to the 1970s as income inequalities were reduced and the welfare state was expanded (Thomas et al., 2010). This historical research suggests that the likely effects of the current policy of austerity in the UK will be to increase health inequalities. We address these interactions of economic and health inequality in more depth in the chapter that follows.

The international perspective: Austerity as structural adjustment

The *Lancet*-University of Oslo Commission on Global Governance for Health, whose report we cited in Chapter 1 (Ottersen et al., 2014), drew a provocative parallel between the conditions attached to the financial rescue packages offered to European countries such as Greece, Ireland and Portugal by the 'troika' of the International Monetary Fund (IMF), the European Commission and the European Central Bank and the structural adjustment conditionalities attached to IMF and World Bank loans to developing countries in the 1980s and 1990s. As early as 1987, a landmark UNICEF study documented the adverse impacts on social determinants of health and argued for an alternative strategy of 'adjustment with a human face' (Cornia et al., 1987). Its findings had little effect on World Bank or IMF policy at the time. In retrospect, it is widely recognized (a) that structural adjustment was at least as much about protecting creditor interests and prying open new markets for direct investment as it was about the well-being of most people in the countries where it was applied; and (b) that the impacts on health were mostly negative (Breman and Shelton, 2007). The picture becomes clearer from an anthropological perspective, describing the destructive effects of structural adjustment on health services and social determinants of health (Pfeiffer and Chapman, 2010).

The appropriateness of the parallel drawn by the *Lancet* Commission is underscored by analysis of the impacts of adjustment policies in the affected countries (Karanikolos et al., 2013; Petmesidou, 2013), and also by the way in which decision-making power has been taken away from the citizens affected by these changes, and assumed instead by 'financial markets' and unaccountable institutions. The failure of political institutions to mount a serious challenge to that shift, despite the damage done by the crisis, is nothing short of remarkable. As the European Trade Union Institute commented in its 2013 annual assessment of the European economy, 'It would seem that we have moved, in the space of four years, from a financial capitalism judged non-compliant with the demands of democracy to a democracy judged non-compliant with the financial markets' (European Trade Union Institute, 2013, p. 7). Structural adjustment as applied to domestic economies need not, however, respond to externally imposed conditionalities or even the 'realities' of globalization; it can also reflect the embrace of neoliberalism by domestic interests and coalitions, and the policies they promote to reorganize economic activity on lines congruent with their 'ideological predilections', to use the phrase quoted earlier. At least one analysis has drawn the analogy between the impacts of IMF and World Bank conditionalities and those of US welfare reform (Schleiter and Statham, 2002), noting that welfare reform expanded the pool of women available for low-wage, insecure jobs they had little alternative but to accept.

Especially when the rhetoric of inevitability is used, as in the UK context, to justify policies that have not achieved the stated objective of deficit reduction, it may be useful to consider austerity from the perspective of human rights – specifically, economic and social rights – in keeping with an international human rights framework that has been suggested as a challenge to market fundamentalism's effects on health (Schrecker et al., 2010). In 2013, the then-high commissioner of human rights of the United Nations argued that austerity measures undertaken in order to reduce deficits had destructive impacts on rights guaranteed under the International Covenant on Economic, Social and Cultural Rights – ratified by most countries, although not by the US. She argued that such measures were only justifiable from a human rights perspective under six conditions: the existence of a compelling state interest; the necessity, reasonableness, temporariness and proportionality of the measures; the exhaustion of alternative and less restrictive measures; non-discriminatory application; maintenance of a 'minimum core content' of affected rights; and genuine participation of those affected (Pillay, 2013). Neoliberalism 3.0 clearly fails on several of these counts – a point that was made in 2013 by the UN special rapporteur on the right to housing with regard to the bedroom tax (Rolnik, 2013). The lack of formal or informal sanctioning processes (in most jurisdictions) for responding to violations of economic and social rights limits their value in concrete strategies for resistance, but they are nevertheless important as a way of re-creating what might be called a political imaginary: the 'right to have rights' independent of the market place that Margaret Somers, whom we cited in Chapter 1, identifies as being called into question by neoliberalism. Inequalities in rights are but one aspect of another neoliberal epidemic: inequality. This is the subject of our next chapter.

5
Inequality: How Politics Divides and Rules Us

Why care about inequality? Within the small local authority area of Stockton-on-Tees (population 192,000), the difference in male life expectancy between the most and least deprived areas in 2014 was 16 years – the highest in England (Public Health England, 2014) and comparable to the difference in national average male life expectancy between the UK and Russia, according to the most recent available World Bank data (World Bank, 2014). A famous map of London's Jubilee underground line shows a decline in life expectancy of more than one year for every two stops as one travels eastward from Westminster (London Health Observatory, 2010). Marmot noted in 2004 that male life expectancy rises 'about a year and a half' for each mile travelled along the Washington, DC metro from the poor (and predominantly black) south east of the city to wealthy, and overwhelmingly white, sub-urban Maryland. The gap in this case was 20 years, comparable at the time to the difference between Kazakhstan and Japan (Marmot, 2004). A review of health inequalities in England led by Marmot, as one of the follow-ups to the report of his WHO Commission (see Chapter 1), pointed out that in 1999–2003 the difference in life expectancy between people living in the most income-deprived neighbourhoods was seven years – and we must keep in mind that the difference within small areas like Stockton-on-Tees is considerably greater – and that the national difference in disability-free life expectancy was much larger, at 17 years. 'So, people in poorer areas not only die sooner, but they will also spend more of their shorter lives with a disability' (Strategic Review, 2010, pp. 16–17; see Figure 5.1). Research using more recent data sets showed that by 2007, which is to say before the financial crisis and subsequent austerity programs, differences in the likelihood of death before age 65 between the 10 per cent of local authority districts with the highest and

87

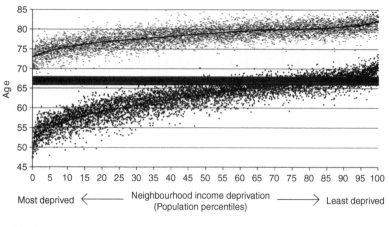

Figure 5.1   Life expectancy and disability-free life expectancy at birth, persons by neighbourhood income level, England, 1999–2003
Source: Reproduced from Strategic Review of Health Inequalities in England post-2010 (2010) *Fair Society, Healthy Lives: The Marmot Review* (London: The Marmot Review) under the Open Government Licence v.3.0. Data from Office of National Statistics, Life Expectancy at Birth, http://www.statistics.gov.uk/StatBase/Product.asp?vlnk=12964 (last accessed 20 November 2014).

lowest prevalence of poverty were larger than at any point since before the Great Depression (Thomas et al., 2010).

The claim is not, of course, that living in a deprived area will actually cause you to live a shorter life – although that might be the case, because of exposures to violence or environmental pollutants. Rather, location – as influenced in the first instance by the sociospatial sorting mechanism of private housing markets – reflects an outcome of material and psychosocial advantage and disadvantage, as they accumulate over the life course (see generally Bartley, 2004, pp. 78–115). A variety of factors can influence or mediate the socioeconomic gradient in health, but its near-ubiquity on multiple scales, within societies rich and poor alike, suggests the importance of the underlying social and economic 'substrate'. To the extent that neoliberalism tends to increase inequality, which is our central theme in this chapter, there is clearly reason for concern. In this chapter, we first describe the major trends in, and drivers of, increasing economic inequality, adding to the picture that emerged in preceding chapters. We proceed to make more explicit the connection with neoliberalism by going beyond macro-scale trends to examine some specific case examples: spatial inequalities in England; incarceration in the US; and neoliberalism and the English health service. At the end of the chapter, we examine an expanding body of evidence that suggests a connection between inequality and health outcomes, not only within communities and societies, but also across them (Wilkinson and Pickett, 2010).

The inequality epidemic: Drivers and trends

In her speech to the 2014 annual joint meeting of the World Bank and the International Monetary Fund, the Fund's managing director described the growth in inequality worldwide as 'staggering' (Lagarde, 2014). Its dimensions in the US and the UK certainly merit that characterization. In 2014, it was reported that the combined wealth of the 104 richest individuals living in the UK amounted to more than £301 billion (BBC News, 2014), and that the wealth of the UK's five richest families alone exceeded the net worth of the bottom 20 per cent of the population (£28.2 billion vs. £28.1 billion; see Dransfield, 2014). In the US, a trend towards increased concentration of wealth at the very top of the economic scale, which was a central finding of Thomas Piketty's (2014) magisterial *Capital in the Twenty-First Century*, was found late in the year to be continuing: based on a wider variety of sources than previous studies, the share of the nation's wealth of the top *0.1 per cent* (one-thousandth) of the population was found to have increased from 7 per cent in 1978 to 22 per cent in 2012 – comparable to the inequality of distribution before the Great Depression, and roughly equal to the net worth of the bottom 90 per cent of the population, which had fallen from 35 per cent in the mid-1980s to 23 per cent (Saez and Zucman, 2014).

Taking a slightly broader view, and looking at income rather than wealth, '[m]ore than 15 percent of US national income was shifted from the bottom 90 percent to the top 10 percent in the United States', and primarily to the top 1 per cent, between 1976 and 2007 (Piketty and Saez, 2013, p. 458). A 2011 OECD study (OECD, 2011) found that income inequality had increased between the mid-1980s and the late 2000s in most high-income countries, interestingly including the Nordic countries (Denmark, Finland, Norway and Sweden) with social democratic welfare states, but not in all (France, Hungary and Belgium were the exceptions). The measure used was the Gini coefficient, a widely used indicator that varies between zero (complete equality) and one (complete inequality). Gini coefficients among the high-income countries in the late 2000s varied from 0.38 in the US (the highest among the high-income countries) to 0.25 in Norway and Denmark. In middle-income Mexico, the Gini coefficient in the late 2000s was estimated at 0.48 (OECD, 2011, p. 45) and in South African cities such as Johannesburg, which are widely recognized as having one of the world's most unequal income distributions, Gini coefficients as high as 0.75 have been estimated (United Nations Human Settlements Program (UN-HABITAT), 2008, p. 73). Gini coefficients for wealth are considerably higher than for income; the Gini coefficient for wealth in the US, for example, has been over 0.80 since the early 1980s (Wolff, 2014).

Like other studies (e.g. Thompson and Smeeding, 2013 on the US), the OECD report concluded that much of the growth in inequality was related to increasing inequality in labour incomes (wages and salaries), and, especially in the US, the UK and Canada, to increases in the incomes of the top 1 per cent of earners. This trend had previously been described as the rise of the 'working rich' (Duménil and Lévy, 2004), and must be understood in conjunction with the expansion of low-wage, precarious work described in Chapter 2. Indeed, in her work on global cities Saskia Sassen (2001) suggested a connection that operates by way of labour markets, as high-wage managers and professionals generate demand for legions of low-wage service workers to drive the taxis, serve or deliver restaurant orders, care for children and clean the buildings. Beyond its focus on employment incomes, the OECD study was cautious in advancing explanations, but did stress that '[r]eforming tax and benefit policies is the most direct and powerful instrument for increasing redistributive effects' (OECD, 2011, p. 40), thus underscoring our emphasis on the importance of politics.

The OECD study could not take into account the effects of the post-2008 recession, and there are several reasons to think that this will increase inequality, in particular in the US and the UK. As Clark and Heath (2014, p. 54) put it in an extensive study of the recession's impact in those countries, 'a pre-existing class divide is *always* inflamed by hard times'. Data from the US show that the unemployment impact of recession was unevenly distributed, with officially measured unemployment having risen by 2010 to more than 17 per cent among workers with less than high school education, and more than 12 per cent among workers with only high school education, compared with less than 4 per cent among those with advanced degrees (Thompson and Smeeding, 2013, pp. 206–209). These are, of course, those workers least likely to have financial resources to tide them over. The recession also 'drove several measures of [hourly] wage inequality to 30-year highs in 2010' in the US (Thompson and Smeeding, 2013, p. 209), again with those workers with lower levels of education most severely affected. In the UK, a similar, although less dramatic, pattern was evident, but unemployment among younger workers (under 24) rose to roughly four times the rate among workers aged 36 and over – a markedly larger gap, and a higher overall youth unemployment rate, than in the US (Clark and Heath, 2014, pp. 54–59). This occurred against a background in which, by 2012, the average real wages of those who remained in work were lower for the bottom tenth of the labour force (in terms of earnings) than in 1979, while the wages of those in the top tenth, despite a substantial post-crisis drop, were still more than 50 per cent higher than in 1979 (Clark and Heath, 2014, p. 77). In the US, real hourly wages for the bottom tenth were 4 per cent lower in 2011 than in 1979, while the top tenth had seen an increase of 30 per cent. The proportion of US workers earning an hourly wage insufficient to support a family of four at the official (and remarkably ungenerous) poverty line was 30 per cent in 1973, and remained at 28 per cent in 2011 (Mishel et al., 2012, pp. 186, 192).

US estimates are that the recession sharply increased inequalities in wealth, as well as incomes. After growing for the previous 25 years, median household wealth – the wealth of a household halfway between the top and the bottom of the income distribution – plunged by 47 per cent between 2007 and 2010, to its lowest level since 1969, as wealth gains from home ownership were wiped out (Wolff, 2014). By 2011, one-quarter of all US households had zero or negative wealth, that is, their debts exceeded their assets – up from 15.5 per cent in 1983, a figure that is already unsettling, and 18.6 per cent in the pre-crisis year of 2007 (Pfeffer et al., 2013). The rich, however, recovered rapidly from the crisis (Piketty and Saez, 2013): by 2010 there were more 'high net worth individuals' – that is, individuals with more than US$1 million in financial assets – than in 2007 in nine out of the ten largest metropolitan areas in the US. The tenth was deindustrialized Detroit, which saw only a slight decrease in the number of high net worth individuals (Capgemini, 2011) even while the core city was headed for bankruptcy.

As suggested in the preceding chapter, austerity is likely to increase inequality. A 2013 study examined 173 episodes in which the governments of 17 OECD countries raised taxes and reduced spending ('fiscal consolidation') between 1978 and 2009, and found that such episodes lead to increases in income inequality as measured by the Gini coefficient over both the short term (two years) and the long term (eight years), and to a decline in the share of national income accounted for by wages and salaries (Ball et al., 2013). These are only some indicators of the impact of austerity; they do not take into account the effects of cuts in public services. Importantly, the most severe impact of the recession in the UK is likely to be associated not with the unemployment of the immediate crisis years, but, rather, with the austerity program described in the preceding chapter (Joyce and Sibieta, 2013), the impacts of which have already fallen disproportionately on the poor, deprived areas, the insecurely employed, and those otherwise marginalized in terms of both income losses and service cuts. It is important once again to emphasize the role of public policy. In the UK, and especially in the US, the growth in the income share of the top 1 per cent that began circa 1980 occurred contemporaneously with reductions in the marginal income tax rate for top earners – in the UK, from 83 per cent in 1980 to 40 per cent in 1988 under Thatcher's government[10] ; in the US case, from 70 per cent in 1980 to 35 per cent by 2002, after the 2001 passage of a package of tax cuts promoted by the Republican administration of George W. Bush. It was estimated at the end of the decade that half the increase in after-tax incomes that resulted from the 2001 Bush cuts flowed to the richest 1 per cent of taxpayers (Citizens for Tax Justice, 2009).

This shift may have intergenerational consequences: the deep economic inequality that characterizes neoliberal societies greatly reduces social mobility, leading to structural entrenchment of inequality whereby your parents' income, job and education now determine your own future social position and health to a greater degree than at any point since the Second World War, at least in the UK and the US, where social mobility has declined since 1980 (Blanden et al., 2005; Federal Reserve Bank of Chicago, 2007). The fall in social mobility in the UK, which parallels the rise in neoliberalism, is illustrated by Blanden et al. (2005), who compare two sons born in 1958 and who left school in the 1970s; the parents of one earned twice as much as the parents of the other. The richer son would earn on average 17.5 per cent more in his early thirties than his poorer friend. For two comparable boys born in 1970 and who left school in the 1980s, this advantage increased to 25 per cent. Mechanisms that increase this gap include the skyrocketing cost of higher education in both the UK and the US and, in the UK, the routinization of unpaid internships, which are thoroughly unaffordable for working-class graduates (Jones, 2011, pp. 180–181). A recent report into (the lack of) social mobility in the UK by the Social Mobility and Child Poverty Commission (2014) found, not surprisingly, that there is a stronger relationship between parental background and children's future income in neoliberal Britain and the US than in many other – less neoliberal – countries such as France, Germany or Sweden. This is a national-level perspective. In the next section of the chapter, we explore the consequences of past economic legacies and current policies under neoliberalism via three case studies: of spatial inequalities in health in England, incarceration in the US and the privatization of the English National Health Service (NHS).

Case example 1: Neoliberalism and spatial inequalities – the North–South health divide in England

The North–South divide in England has been a popular trope from the mid-nineteenth century novels of Charles Dickens (*Hard Times*, 1854) and Elizabeth Gaskell (*North and South*, 1855) through to more recent books and broadcast documentaries (Russell, 2004; BBC TV, 2014). For the past four decades, Northern England (commonly defined as the North East, North West and Yorkshire and Humber regions) has persistently had higher mortality rates than the South of England, and the gap has widened over time – particularly during the neoliberal era (Hacking et al., 2011). For example, between 2009 and 2011 people in Manchester (North West) were more than twice as likely to die early as people living in Wokingham (South East) (Public Health England, 2013). This is demonstrated further in Figures 5.2 and 5.3, which show life expectancy by local authority in England for men and women.

Levels of economic deprivation in the North are much higher than in the South (Whitehead and Doran, 2011). While the North represents 30 per cent of the population of England, it includes 50 per cent of the poorest neighbourhoods (local council wards with populations of about 3000 people; Bambra and Garthwaite, 2014). Based on a definition of poverty as the proportion of people living in households with an income below 60 per cent of the median household income – a somewhat more expansive definition, resulting in higher prevalences of poverty, than the one used in Figure 5.1 – the regions with the lowest levels of poverty were the South East (17 per cent) and East (18 per cent) of England. Rates were much higher in the Northern regions, with 22 per cent in the North East, 23 per cent in the North West and 24 per cent in Yorkshire and Humber. Even before the effects of the recession were compounded by austerity, people in the North also had the most debt, owing 34p for every pound in gross income, in contrast to 17p and 12p for the South East and South West, respectively (*Which*, 2012). London, economically the most unequal region in the entire European Union

Male

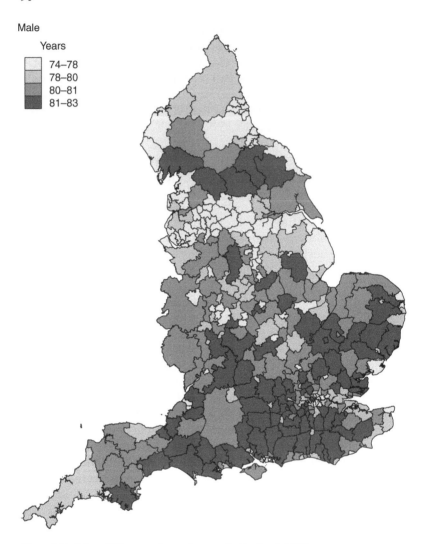

Years

☐ 74–78
☐ 78–80
☐ 80–81
■ 81–83

Figure 5.2 Map of life expectancy for men in England, 2011

Source: Reproduced with the permission of the Centre for Local Economic Strategies from M. Whitehead (Chair), C. Bambra, B. Barr et al., *Due North: Report of the Inquiry on Health Equity for the North* (Liverpool and Manchester: University of Liverpool and Centre for Local Economic Strategies, 2014). Map produced by Ben Barr, University of Liverpool, using data from the Health and Social Care Information Centre.

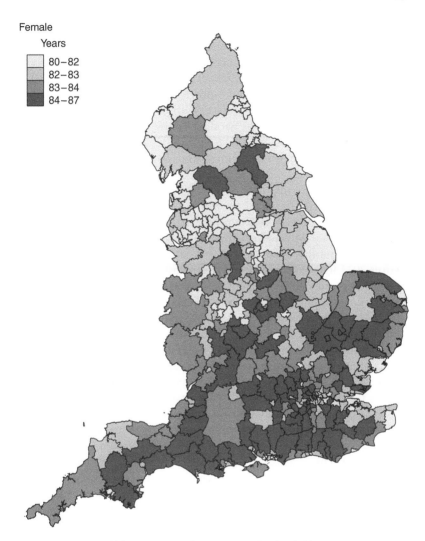

Female

Years

80–82
82–83
83–84
84–87

Figure 5.3 Map of life expectancy for women in England, 2011
Source: Reproduced with the permission of the Centre for Local Economic Strategies from
M. Whitehead (Chair), C. Bambra, B. Barr et al., *Due North: Report of the Inquiry on Health
Equity for the North* (Liverpool and Manchester: University of Liverpool and Centre for Local
Economic Strategies, 2014). Map produced by Ben Barr, University of Liverpool, using data
from the Health and Social Care Information Centre.

(Eurostat, 2014) because of its concentrations of wealth, tops the league table for the highest proportion and number of households devoting more than 25 per cent of their incomes to unsecured debt repayments (10.2 per cent), but it is closely followed by the North East (10.1 per cent) and North West (9.5 per cent). Accordingly, there is a wide regional variation in the demand for debt advice, with debt issues accounting for 46 per cent of all advice cases handled by the Citizens Advice Bureau (CAB) in the North East compared with only 22 per cent of all issues handled by the CAB in the more prosperous South East (Citizens Advice Bureau, 2013).

There are also geographical differences in the availability of social housing (another indicator of deprivation, where high levels of social housing mean higher levels of deprivation) and the proportion of home owners compared with renters. The North East has one of the highest rates of social renting at 23 per cent (the national average is 18 per cent). Census 2011 figures show that the North East also has the second highest level of renters, at 38 per cent compared with the average of 36 per cent for England and Wales. The South East has the lowest levels of renting, at 31 per cent. Among the 8.3 million renters in 2011, those renting from private landlords or letting agents were up 1.7–3.6 million compared to 2001, while those socially renting decreased by about 100,000 to 4.1 million. In a context where increasing numbers of households are facing a choice between eating an adequate diet and heating their homes, the North East and North West have some of the highest levels of fuel poverty in England, as shown in Figure 5.4.

Over the past 40 years, the North has consistently had lower employment rates than the South for both men and women (Clark and Heath, 2014, p. 65). This is associated with the lasting effects of deindustrialization in the latter part of the 20th century; with neoliberal economic policies and the abandonment of full employment there were regionally concentrated falls in the demand for labour (most notably in the North East and North West), particularly affecting those with less education (Nickell and Quintini, 2002). These patterns have persisted, resulting in significant regional variations in worklessness and associated poverty and welfare receipt. High rates of unemployment can be found in almost all parts of the North. In 2014, unemployment rates are 9 per cent in the North compared with 7 per cent in the rest of England and 8 per cent in London. Fourteen per cent of the working-age population were receiving key out-of-work benefits (jobseekers allowance; employment and support allowance and incapacity benefit; lone parents; carers; others on income-related benefits; disabled; bereaved), as compared with 10 per

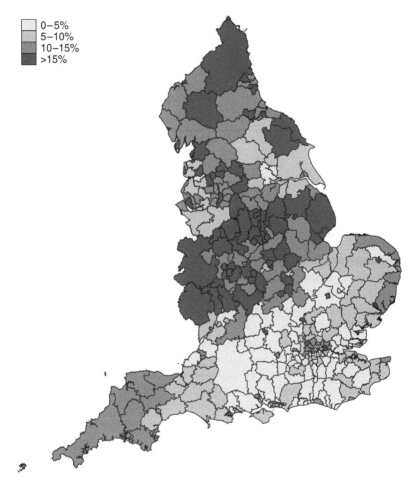

Figure 5.4 Map showing percentage of households experiencing fuel poverty by local authority in England, 2012

Source: Reproduced with the permission of the Centre for Local Economic Strategies from M. Whitehead (Chair), C. Bambra, B. Barr et al., *Due North: Report of the Inquiry on Health Equity for the North* (Liverpool and Manchester: University of Liverpool and Centre for Local Economic Strategies, 2014). Map produced by Ben Barr, University of Liverpool, using data from the Department for Energy and Climate Change (low income high costs definition of fuel poverty).

cent in London and 13 per cent in England as a whole. The North East has the highest rate of 15 per cent, with the North West and Yorkshire and the Humber having 13 per cent and 12 per cent, respectively (Bambra and Garthwaite, 2014). For those who are in work, wages are lower, and the legacy of deindustrialization has resulted in concentrations of worklessness which have persisted for generations, whereby whole families grow up within a community in which work is no longer the norm.

This has resulted in a debate about whether there is a 'culture of worklessness' (Bambra, 2011, pp. 150–152) among benefit recipients, particularly in the North. This constructs 'workless people as those who "won't work", rather than those people for whom there are few jobs to apply for, who face barriers to work, including various and multiple forms of discrimination' (Grover and Piggott, 2007, p. 536). Such characterizations owe much to the 'culture of poverty' debates that emerged in the US in the late 1960s, in which cultural patterns (family structure, interpersonal relations, value systems, sense of community and spending patterns) were seen to be intergenerationally transmitted by the welfare system, resulting in a recurring cycle of poverty and welfare dependency (Fletcher, 2007). These stereotypes were reinvigorated by politicians and commentators on the right in the welfare reform debates of the 1980s and 1990s, and instantiate the individualization of responsibility that is a key element of neoliberalism's ideological dimension, as noted in Chapter 1. However, it is not the welfare system but the macroeconomic environment, deindustrialization, government inaction and the wider system of neoliberal economic and spatial inequality that are really the cause of such intergenerational transmission and long-term social exclusion of deprived communities (Byrne, 2005). There is strong evidence that a substantial proportion of those in receipt of benefits want to return to work and would do so if they were given appropriate support (Bambra, 2011), and there is little evidence of a lower work ethic among workless people (Gallie, 2004).

Case example 2: The epidemic of incarceration in the US

Starting in the early 1970s, rates of imprisonment in the US began to rise, in what sociologist Loïc Wacquant (2009) has called the Great Confinement. In 1972, 161 people out of every 100,000 US residents were incarcerated; in 2012, the rate was 707 per 100,000, a total of more than 2.2 million people – by far the highest rate in the world – and the absolute number of people held in US jails and prisons grew sevenfold (Travis et al., 2014, p. 33). These figures substantially understate the 'reach' of the correctional system; once released from jail or prison, many inmates remain subject to probation or parole, and the numbers of people under such supervision increased from 1.6 million in 1976 to roughly 4.8 million in 2010–2012. Thus, the total number of people under some form of correctional supervision stood at approximately seven million by 2010–2012, with further increases anticipated because of the range of parole and probation violations that trigger re-incarceration (Lin, 2010; Travis et al., 2014, pp. 40–42). The incarceration rate continued to climb through the end of the 20th century before beginning to level out, despite a sharp decline in the frequency of major crimes such as homicide, vehicle theft and burglary (Travis et al., 2014, pp. 27, 46). Perhaps the most striking, and familiar, feature of the pattern of incarceration is the disproportionately high rate at which Hispanics and (especially) African-Americans, most particularly young African-American men, are imprisoned (Travis et al., 2014, pp. 64–68). The percentage of all 20-year-old African-American men imprisoned in the US more than tripled between 1974 and 2004 (Drucker, 2011, p. 101), with those with limited education at especially high risk; '[i]ncredibly, a black male dropout, born in the late 1960s, had nearly a 60 percent chance of serving time in prison by the end of the 1990s' (Western, 2007, p. 517).

The increases in imprisonment were policy-driven, by choices about the targets and intensity of law enforcement and about the length and frequency of prison sentences (Travis et al., 2014, pp. 70–103). At least two key influences can be identified. The first is the lengthening of prison sentences for a range of offences; reduction of judicial flexibility in sentencing through such requirements as mandatory minimum sentences; and measures such as 'three strikes and you're out' statutes mandating life in prison following a third conviction for broad categories of offences (Wacquant, 2009, pp. 65–67; Travis et al., 2014, pp. 71–85). The second is the intensified enforcement of drug prohibitions – the 'War on Drugs', characterized two decades ago by criminologist Diana Gordon (1994) as being in part a mechanism or pretext for controlling new dangerous classes. While other forms of crime declined, rising numbers of drug arrests – which are policy-driven in the sense that they depend on levels of enforcement – combined with stiffer sentencing requirements to swell prison populations. At the state level, the frequency with which people were imprisoned for drug offences increased nearly tenfold between 1980 and 2010; the increase was even greater at the federal level between 1980 and 2000 (Travis et al., 2014, pp. 47–48, 56). The 2014 report of a National Academy of Sciences panel, from which we have drawn many of the statistics for this section of the chapter, supports decades of critique by social scientists and activists with the conclusion: 'Many features of U.S. criminal justice systems – including unwarranted disparities in imprisonment, invidious bias and stereotyping, police drug arrest practices, and racial profiling – disproportionately affect blacks and Hispanics' (Travis et al., 2014, p. 91, citations omitted; see generally 93–101). This can, in turn, be viewed as a reflection that US crime policy, like many other aspects of public policy (including welfare reform), has reflected racial antagonisms and efforts by politicians to appeal to racial stereotypes since the 1960s (Travis et al., 2014, pp. 109–121).

Nothing is especially new about these observations. What justifies our characterization of the sevenfold growth in imprisonment rates as a neoliberal epidemic? Some elements of the trend may be driven by broader economic developments: in deindustrialized cities hard-hit by factory closings, the drug economy may for a time have represented a primary urban survival strategy (Tourigny, 2001; Bourgois, 2003) for those who lacked the credentials or resources to find work elsewhere. At least in the case of New York City, the effects of structural economic change were magnified by the adoption of policies of 'benign neglect' (a phrase used by an advisor to President Nixon) and 'planned shrinkage' (used by an advisor to the New York City government) (Wallace and Wallace, 1998, pp. 21–77). The consequences included epidemics of fires, large-scale population displacements and the disintegration of what had been stable, if poor, communities. This example of cost-cutting contrasts with the seemingly limitless public resources that were available to expand prisons, at least until the financial crisis and its aftermath, even while public sector budgets in other areas were being squeezed. If corrections had been a single employer, by the end of the 20th century it would have been the third largest employer in the US, behind only Manpower Inc., a temporary employment agency and Wal-Mart (Wacquant, 2009, pp. 151–165). Indeed, rather like health care, prisons have themselves become a growth industry involving large private corporations as well as powerful unions in some states, which function as important constituencies for further expansion (Christie, 1993, pp. 93–126; Wacquant, 2009, pp. 64–65; Travis et al., 2014, p. 126). Privatized probation supervision has recently emerged as a new profit centre, and the fact that the corporations in question are legally empowered to recover costs directly from their 'clients' (Albin-Lackey, 2014) contributes to the vicious downward cycle of incarceration and impoverishment.

The size of the crime control and corrections industry contributes to the persistent and self-sustaining character of the growth in imprisonment, which is central to epidemiologist Ernest Drucker's (2011) characterization of the trend as an epidemic. The epidemic is self-sustaining in several other ways, as well, which, in addition to the involvement of a large and profitable industry, are central to our characterization of the epidemic as neoliberal. The growth in imprisonment ratchets up inequality (Western, 2007), magnifying existing class and racial disparities in the incidence of imprisonment quite apart from the frequently inhumane conditions of prison life itself (see e.g. Winerip and Schwirtz, 2014), increasingly involving long periods of solitary confinement (Drucker, 2011, pp. 128–129). People in certain disadvantaged geographical areas are especially likely to go to prison, and the impact on the social fabric of those communities may actually increase crime (Clear, 2007). By the mid-1990s, urbanist Edward Goetz (1996) argued that the War on Drugs represented the US' *de facto* urban policy, one that abandoned concern for cities as viable communities and prioritized the containment of subaltern urban populations.[11]

For individuals, some of the most profound consequences unfold post-sentence. The psychological adaptations needed to survive in prison may be thoroughly dysfunctional on the 'outside' (Travis et al., 2014, p. 194). Being on parole or probation, or just having a criminal record, seriously limits employment opportunities (Emsellem and Mukamal, 2008; Travis et al., 2014, pp. 237–239), creating economic constraints that may be compounded by restrictions on access to public housing and income support; many of these limitations reflect provisions of the welfare reform legislation of 1996, discussed in the preceding chapter (Wacquant, 2009, pp. 82–87, 135–146; Drucker, 2011, pp. 129–137). A substantial number of the more than *7.6 million* inmates released from jail or prison each year in recent years end up precariously housed or homeless, which increases risks of re-incarceration (Drucker, 2011, pp. 131–134; Dumont et al., 2011, p. 331). Drucker describes the cumulative effect of these impacts as 'chronic incapacitation' that may be lifelong. Importantly, the epidemic affects not only those millions of people imprisoned, but also their families and children (Drucker, 2011, pp. 141–162; Travis et al., 2014, pp. 260–277), creating the likelihood of intergenerational transmission of economic vulnerability and risk of imprisonment that is, like the initial impacts of the epidemic, likely to be heavily concentrated among the disadvantaged. As in the case of current retrenchments of social policy (austerity) worldwide, the epidemic of incarceration in the US represents a large-scale neoliberal social experiment, the health consequences of which would take some time to play out even if the policies that sustain the epidemic were to be changed immediately.

Wacquant (2009) goes further. In a major expansion of the line of argument advanced by Goetz and others, he views welfare reform, in particular the combination of shrinking or non-existent benefits with 'workfare' requirements, and the expansion of incarceration as functionally related elements of a fundamental neoliberal reconstitution of the state that expands social and economic insecurity, including expanding the pool of low-wage labour, while expanding the coercive capabilities of the state that are exemplified by prisons. To oversimplify a complex argument, for Wacquant this reconstitution is characterized by four 'institutional logics' – economic deregulation, welfare state retrenchment, 'the cultural trope of individual responsibility' and an expanded penal apparatus that is *required* for the control of an impoverished and, at least in the US context, racialized population (pp. 307–308) – a stratum he characterizes as a subproletariat (pp. 69–75). The expanded criminalization of poverty in the US since the original (French-language, 2004) publication of Wacquant's book, directly and in the form of expanded use of police and criminal sanctions for what would previously have been regarded as minor breaches of public order, closely tied to marginal economic status (Beckett and Herbert, 2009; Ehrenreich, 2009), arguably confirms his diagnosis. On the other hand, much of his argument is drawn from the experience of the US, which may reflect a unique set of domestic political circumstances and institutions and a distinctively virulent strain of neoliberalism. His concern about the export of the US model to France (pp. 270–286) is motivated by a conviction that carceral expansion is unavoidably associated with neoliberalism. If he is correct, then we can expect it to manifest in other jurisdictions that continue down the road of neoliberal economic and social policies.

Case example 3: Neoliberalism and the privatization and marketization of the English National Health Service

In Chapter 1 we introduced the concept of social determinants of health, and in this book we concentrate on neoliberalism's influence on the unequal distribution of these determinants as a cause of ill health. However, health care systems have also been affected. Over the last 25 years, the health care systems of most high-income countries have experienced extensive – often market-based – organizational and financial reforms. This section provides a case study of the potential effects of such reforms on health inequalities using a study of the NHS in England.

Publicly financed health care that covers an entire population, without regard for ability to pay, is a buffer against some of the worst consequences of the risk shift, and, especially when financed from general tax revenues, has a substantial redistributive effect, as the wealthy and healthy in effect subsidize the treatment of the less healthy and poorer – in the extreme, those who are unable to work, and, of course, those past the age when they should be expected to. This redistributive function at least partly accounts for the attacks that have been associated with neoliberalization (Evans, 1987, 1997). Britain's NHS was founded in 1948 as a single national health system funded from general tax revenues, free at the point of use, ultimately accountable to the national government but run by local health boards. It has never been the only provider of health care, with some wealthy individuals either paying for care directly or moving to the head of the queue through private insurance – a choice historically made only by about 5 per cent of the population, but one that is actively, and increasingly, promoted by the health insurance industry.

In 1992, the publication of Osborne and Gaebler's *Reinventing Government* catalysed interest in the New Public Management, which promoted competition in the provision of public services and the introduction of private sector management techniques, purportedly in the name of increasing efficiency and reducing costs (Hood, 1991; Shields and Evans, 1998, pp. 71–87). An important conceptual shift involved regarding the users of public services as customers, rather than citizens. The NHS had already been targeted for market-based reforms, when an internal market – an idea imported from US health care management theory (Pollock, 2004, pp. 41–46, 102–108, 198) – was first introduced in 1989 by the Conservative government. In 1991 the Conservative government imported another management nostrum, the purchaser–provider split, into the organization of local health systems under the NHS and Community Care Act (1990). It created two models of commissioning (the purchase of services under contractual arrangements) – one based on health authorities, and the other, general practitioner (GP) fundholding, based on general practice. The effect was actually to increase NHS privatization and will lead, and indeed has already led, to increases in the proportion of the NHS budget devoted to administration, as the number of senior managers multiplied, while increasing inequalities in provision, resulting in a 'postcode lottery' in which access and quality varied depending on the locally contracted provider (Pollock, 2004, pp. 19–49). In 1997, the New Labour government abolished GP fundholding but retained the purchaser–provider split and, after 2002, sought to further strengthen the internal market and shift the balance of power in the NHS from the providers of care (e.g. hospitals) to the purchasers (health care commissioners) via a variety of measures (Hunter, 2008). Among them:

- Private providers, called Diagnostic and Treatment Centres and later Independent Treatment Centres, started to be used to provide NHS services to reduce waiting lists (Pollock, 2004, pp. 68–71). Although the NHS remained in theory the 'preferred provider', there were issues with the quality of care provided by these services and the cherry-picking of lower-cost, easier-to-treat patients (see Leys and Player, 2011).
- Public–private partnerships under the Private Finance Initiative (PFI) were used to fund the redevelopment of existing NHS hospitals and to build new ones via funding public infrastructure projects with private capital. However, significant concerns emerged over the long-term financial costs to the public purse of these programs (Pollock, 2004, pp. 52–58; Leys and Player, 2011).
- Practice-based commissioning: a new form of GP fundholding whereby GPs commissioned services for their patients, albeit under the supervision of larger, geographically based Primary Care Trusts.
- Foundation Trusts, a form of reorganization that enabled hospitals to become independent corporations, non-profit but operated – indeed, mandated to operate – along commercial lines, with limited accountability to either the communities they serve or the national health ministry (Pollock, 2004, pp. 71–73, 123–124).
- Payment by results: payments for health services (e.g. operations) based on standardized tariffs for average costs. This departed from the prior arrangement whereby hospitals were given a global budget based on historical usage and expenditure. Among the risks here is that such a funding scheme creates disincentives to treat poorer patients, who often represent more complicated cases with multiple co-morbidities complicated by their life situations (Pollock, 2004, pp. 73–75).

In 2010, the Conservative-led coalition government embarked upon a further program of reform, resulting in the 2012 *Health and Social Care Act* (for a thorough overview of the implications of the legislation see Davis and Tallis, 2013). This sought to transform the NHS from a publicly provided service to one that enabled full private competition from 'any qualified provider' with services commissioned by Clinical Commissioning Groups (CCGs) of GPs. Among other consequences, this has opened up the English NHS to the full thrust of EU competition law

(Reynolds, 2011), resulting in multi-million-pound NHS service contracts being awarded to large private, for-profit service providers such as Circle (Europe's largest healthcare partnership, which in January 2015 withdrew from a contract to run Hinchingbrooke Hospital Healthcare NHS Trust, the UK's first NHS hospital run by a private company) and Virgin Health. The 'opening up [of] the whole of the NHS supply system' that then-Prime Minister Blair had envisioned in 2003 (quoted in Pollock, 2004, p. 69) had seemingly been accomplished a decade later, when it was reported that US defence supplier Lockheed Martin was in the running for a £1 billion contract to provide support services for GP practices (Cooper, 2014).

Some evidence suggests that opening up the lucrative NHS market to private providers was, in fact, an intended consequence of the reforms (Reynolds et al., 2011). Despite criticisms of NHS quality of care, a few high-profile scandals and recurrent alarms about insufficient funding, in the Commonwealth Fund's 2014 annual survey of health system performance the NHS ranked first among the health systems of 11 high-income countries, despite being one of the least costly on a per capita basis (Davis et al., 2014). In the wake of a 2014 investigation by *The Times* of problems introduced by the 2012 reorganization, including billions of pounds paid for overpriced supplies, unusable drugs and high-priced temporary contractors, senior government sources were quoted as saying that it was 'the biggest mistake they have made in government', and, indeed, was never understood by the prime minister (Smyth et al., 2014). One of the arguments put forward by proponents of NHS marketization and privatization was that choice and competition in health care would increase patient choice, quality of services and equity in access to services, and therefore reduce health inequalities (Le Grand, 2007, p. 42). Conversely, an abundant body of critique has suggested that the recommodifying influence (Pollock, 2004, pp. 16–17) of NHS 'reforms' has degraded quality of care and equality of access while failing to deliver promised organizational 'efficiencies'.

Although the *potential* effects of health care marketization and privatization on equity have been highlighted by both supporters and opponents of NHS reform, it was only recently that systematic comparative research into their *actual* effects on health equity was conducted. One of us, along with colleagues (Bambra et al., 2014), examined studies of the effects of such reforms on health equity in developed country health care systems.[12] This research found that reforms that increased private insurance and out-of-pocket payments, as well as the marketization and privatization of services, had either negative or inconclusive effects on equity, both in terms of access relative to health need and in terms of actual health outcomes. For example, a French study (Bellanger and Mosse, 2005) found that increases in the role of private insurance had negative effects on health equity, as between 1980 and 2003, when the public share of health care expenditure decreased and private insurance increased, social and spatial inequalities in access to health care increased, particularly in relation to preventative, perinatal and sexual health services. Similarly, a Swedish study (Burström, 2002) found that the increase in service user fees (e.g. paying to see a GP) as a result of the early 1990s health care reforms led to an increase in the proportion of lower-income people reporting that they had 'needed but not sought medical care' after the reforms (1996–1997) than before (1988–1989). This was accompanied by an increased utilization of emergency care by lower-income groups. An Italian study (Donia Sofio, 2006) also found that an increase in the role of out-of-pocket payments for health services in the 2000s led to the impoverishment of 1.3 per cent of Italian households – a trend that we can anticipate will become more pronounced in the aftermath of the fiscal crisis and subsequent austerity measures. This negative impact on income distribution was largely as a result of pharmaceutical, specialist and dental services. A study of the internal market in primary care in England (GP fundholding) found negative impacts on equity of access (Mannion, 2005). Another English study of patient choice found that lower-educated and low-income groups were less likely to exercise their right to choose a provider, for example by choosing an alternative hospital (Coulter et al., 2005).

A concern being mooted at the time of writing (late 2014) is that investor-state dispute settlement (ISDS) provisions in the Transatlantic Trade and Investment Partnership (TTIP) agreement now under negotiation could require provision of health services to be opened up to private, for-profit providers in any signatory country (including other EU countries and the US), exposing the UK government to huge liabilities for lost profits were it subsequently to bring contracted-out services back under the control of the NHS (Hilary, 2014). Such an outcome would be entirely consistent with the view of some commentators that a key purpose of such agreements is to lock in or 'constitutionalize' cross-border access to investment opportunities (Schneiderman, 2008). A further illustration of the destructive effects of private provision and financing, which by now needs little elaboration, is provided by the long-standing problems of the uninsured in the US, the high-income country that has long had the most market-based approach to health care and also, not coincidentally, by far the highest health care costs, per person and as a percentage of GDP. While the NHS scored highest on that 2014 Commonwealth Fund survey, the US scored 'last overall, and last or close to last on four of the five dimensions of a high performance health system, including health outcomes' (Davis et al., 2014, p. 12). Despite the 2010 Patient Protection and Affordable Care Act (ObamaCare), the most recent estimate available at the time of writing was that, in 2013, 42 million people, or 13.4 per cent of the population, were without health insurance for the entire calendar year (Velkoff, 2014). A larger number of people were uninsured for part of the year, perhaps because of job loss. Many millions more had inadequate or incomplete coverage, with health care or health insurance costs and the earnings losses associated with illness contributing to a substantial proportion of personal bankruptcies. While the unemployed or unemployable and the working poor rely on emergency rooms to deal with acute illnesses that would be avoidable given an adequate system of primary health care for all (Reynolds, 2010), private, for-profit providers have demonstrated extraordinary resourcefulness in seeking to maintain and increase their income streams, with hospitals keeping the insured terminally ill alive as long as possible in order to get maximum returns from insurance (Brill, 2013; Creswell et al., 2014; Rosenthal, 2014). This is the unavoidable outcome when health care and health insurance operate as industries, and the neoliberal project as applied to the NHS runs the very real risk of importing this toxic and inequitable model into the UK.

Is less inequality better for (almost) everyone?

Our discussion so far has addressed how inequality is likely to result in differences in opportunities to be healthy among members of a particular society. A separate and increasingly compelling body of research, which complements and supports our earlier discussion of the health effects of different welfare regimes, finds that societies that are more unequal may have worse health outcomes *on average*. In other words, there is a socioeconomic gradient among countries that is defined by their levels of economic inequality. In *The Spirit Level*, epidemiologists Richard Wilkinson and Kate Pickett (2010, pp. 73–87) summarize an extensive body of evidence that life expectancy and infant mortality are correlated with the level of income inequality across high-income countries (with inequality measured by the ratio of incomes of the top 20 per cent of the population to the bottom 20 per cent; see Figures 5.5 and 5.6) and, within the US, across states (with income measured by

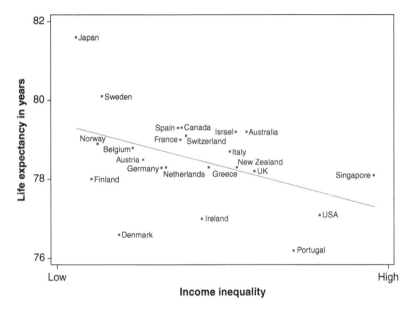

Figure 5.5   Life expectancy is related to inequality in rich countries
Source: Wilkinson, R. and Pickett, K. *The Spirit Level: Why Equality is Better for Everyone* (London: Penguin), reproduced with permission.

Gini coefficient at the state level). Considerable variation exists among countries and states at any level of income inequality, reflecting the effects of other, context-specific influences, but the trend is clear. More unequal jurisdictions tend to have higher infant mortality and lower life expectancy. Similarly, more unequal countries, and more unequal US states, tend to have higher rates of adult obesity and child overweight – again with considerable variation, as we would expect given the multiple influences on overweight and obesity (see Chapter 2). A similar pattern exists among US states for mortality rates from a number of major causes of disease studied separately, with mortality inversely related to county-level median income *but also*, for some causes of death, to state-level income inequality (Wilkinson and Pickett, 2008). A separate systematic review of cohort studies that included a total of 60 million participants found that living in a country with high income inequality is associated with an excess risk of premature mortality, independently of individual characteristics (Kondo et al., 2009).

The relationship also seems to exist for income inequality in smaller areas: a study of mortality among the working-age (25–64) population in 528 metropolitan areas in Canada, the US, Australia, Sweden and Britain

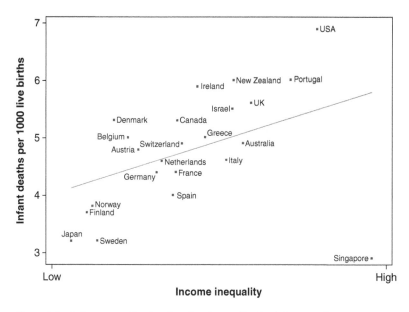

Figure 5.6   Infant mortality is related to inequality in rich countries
Source: Wilkinson, R. and Pickett, K. *The Spirit Level: Why Equality is Better for Everyone* (London: Penguin), reproduced with permission.

found a clear association between intra-metropolitan income inequality (as measured by median share of household income) and higher levels of mortality, both for the sample of metropolitan areas as a whole and for cities in the US and Britain, the two countries with the most unequal intra-metropolitan distributions of income, although not for those in the other countries (Ross et al., 2005b). Wilkinson and Pickett observed similar inequality-related gradients both across countries and within the US for other outcomes, including educational performance, frequency of teenage births, homicide rates and imprisonment rates.

What could account for this gradient? We return to the question of causal complexity that we introduced in Chapter 1. Multiple mechanisms are probably involved, and it is not claimed that economic inequality is the only influence on health. It is significant that, when Wilkinson and Pickett combined multiple indicators[13] into a composite index of health and social problems, they found a very close relation to inequality (Figure 5.7). This would suggest that a common element is at work that involves something about the overall organization of the society. Ross et al. (2005a, p. 219) have made a similar observation about the findings on the relation between intra-metropolitan income

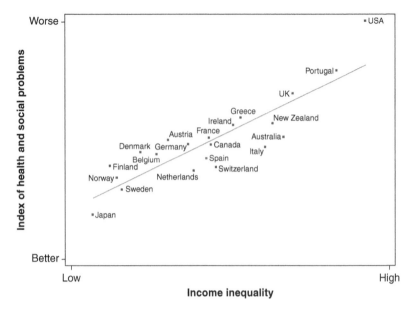

Figure 5.7   Health and social problems are closely related to inequality among rich countries
Source: Wilkinson, R. and Pickett, K. *The Spirit Level: Why Equality is Better for Everyone* (London: Penguin), reproduced with permission.

inequality and working-age mortality, speculating (for example) that greater concentrations of affluence and poverty in US cities may explain part of the difference between the US and Canada (Ross et al., 2005a, pp. 226–229); they did not examine this variable for the UK cities, which also exhibited an inequality-related gradient in mortality. For health outcomes, a key factor would appear to be the biological consequences of social position, which, as we saw from our earlier discussion of the Whitehall studies, is related to a variety of health outcomes in ways that are not explicable by material deprivation. Wilkinson and Pickett (2010, p. 87) conclude: 'The biology of chronic stress is a plausible pathway which helps us to understand why unequal societies are almost always unhealthy societies.'

We discussed that pathway in the context of work environments and economic insecurity in chapters 2 and 3. Two studies in the US used national health survey data to generate allostatic load scores (recall that allostatic load is a measure of the biological effects of stress), including such indicators as systolic and diastolic blood pressure and blood levels of high density lipoproteins and total cholesterol, to assess the overall impact of what have been referred to as different epidemiological worlds (Rydin et al., 2012). Geronimus et al. (2006) separated the population by race (black and white), by gender and into poor and non-poor based on household incomes. They found that allostatic load scores rose with age for all groups, but being poor, being black and being female each operated independently to increase the probability of a high score, and 'in each age group the mean score for Blacks was roughly comparable to that for Whites who were 10 years older'. Bird et al. (2010), using allostatic load scores derived from the same national data, found that 'significantly greater biological wear and tear' was associated with living in census tracts where socioeconomic status was lower, independently of individual characteristics like race and economic status. The message is clear: whether defined by discrimination along the multiple axes of gender and race, by individual poverty or by living in disadvantaged areas – and these forms of disadvantage tend to co-occur – low social position tends to wear you out over time in biologically measurable ways. Given neoliberalism's tendency to increase economic inequality, the implications for public health are, to say the least, far-reaching. We explore ways to address these implications in the concluding chapter.

6

Conclusion: Their Scarcity and Our Political Cure

In our concluding chapter, we outline some common themes shared across the four neoliberal epidemics that we have identified, offering some reflections on the evidence of the ill-health effects of neoliberalism and the likely intergenerational transmission of neoliberal epidemics. We conclude the book by outlining alternative views of the future of health – both pessimistic and optimistic – arguing that these neoliberal epidemics require a political cure.

Evidence and inertia: Why have the neoliberal epidemics been ignored?

So, what is to be done if we are to prevent the spread and entrenchment of neoliberal epidemics? If you have read this far, it will be unsurprising to you that we advocate radical changes to politics, economy and society – returning Neoliberalism 3.0 to the publisher for replacement with a more suitable product, as it were. This means, first of all, rejecting the sort of 'sticking plasters' usually recommended in the mainstream – such as diet clubs for the obese, financial education or credit counselling for those in debt, cognitive behavioural therapy for those experiencing stress or more healthy lifestyles for those on the wrong side of the inequality divide. These are wholly inadequate, and sometimes constitute impediments to serious efforts to reduce health inequalities by legitimizing the neoliberal ascription of primary responsibility for health to individuals and their 'lifestyles' (Schrecker, 2013a). The causes of these epidemics are political, economic and social. They are not the fault of individuals, and in many cases are entirely out of their control; think of the financial crisis and its consequences.

Some readers, and not a few academic colleagues, will object that we have not presented an adequately evidence-based case against neoliberalism. Epidemiologists often object to the inference of causation from 'simple ecologic correlation studies' as opposed to findings from experimental studies such as randomized controlled trials (RCTs) or quasi-experimental designs (Kaufman and Harper, 2013). This perspective is favourable to the (neoliberal) status quo, whether or not by intention. Given the increasing demand that both medical practice and health policy should be evidence-based, while in other areas of public life policy is often made on flimsy evidence, or in the face of the available evidence, several responses are in order.

In Chapter 2, we explained the complexity of influences on obesity. These exemplify the kinds of influences on health that 'involve multiple complex and lengthy pathways, making it much more difficult to study the effectiveness of social conditions under controlled conditions' (Braveman et al., 2011, p. S60, see generally S60–S61) using experimental or (usually) even quasi-experimental designs for reasons of ethics, logistics or both. RCTs in particular, the gold standard for research on clinical interventions, are of limited relevance because of the inability to control for all variables but one; in the real worlds of people's lives, many things are going on at once (Woolf and Aron, 2013, pp. 164, 262–263). The other highly regarded form of study design, the longitudinal prospective cohort study (such as the Whitehall studies), raises a slightly different problem: the need to wait years, if not decades, for findings – an effect that has been described as 'epidemiological inertia' (Frank and Haw, 2011). In order to get around this problem, one option is to accept evidence of causal relations between policies or interventions and risk factors for adverse health outcomes, like overweight or increased allostatic load, rather than adverse outcomes themselves as sufficient to justify policy change. Even this may not cast the net widely enough. As noted in a recent literature review on adult overweight and obesity,

> many strategies aimed at obesity prevention may not be expected to have a direct impact on BMI, but rather on pathways that will alter the context in which eating, physical activity and weight control occur. Any restriction on the concept of a successful outcome, to either weight-maintenance or BMI measures alone, is therefore likely to overlook many possible intervention measures that could contribute to obesity prevention.
>
> (Mooney et al., 2011, p. 22)

Natural experiments – comparing outcomes in countries that have made different political choices or implemented different policies – are a viable alternative (and a method that we have drawn upon in this book; see Barr et al., forthcoming).

These issues all relate to what in law would be called the choice of a standard of proof: deciding on how much evidence is enough to reach a conclusion – for example, of guilt in a criminal case, or of liability for damages in a civil suit. Importantly, this is not a scientific question and cannot be answered by the methods of science *qua* science. As the legal analogy suggests, it requires value judgements about how, and in whose interests, uncertainty should be resolved (Schrecker, 2013b). It is possible to make the standard of proof for acting on social determinants of health sufficiently demanding that the evidence can never be good enough. Our view is that this is counterproductive and even unethical from a public health perspective, given both the possible costs of inaction on some of the epidemics we have described and the unequal and inequitable distribution of those costs. To quote Marmot, '[T]he best should not be the enemy of the good. While we should not formulate policies in the absence of evidence to support them, we must not be paralyzed into inaction while we wait for the evidence to be absolutely unimpeachable' (Marmot, 2000, p. 308). Developing public health policy requires assembling evidence of various kinds that, when taken together, tells a convincing causal story, while keeping in mind the costs of resolving uncertainty by waiting for the epidemiological Godot of more research (Braveman et al., 2011, pp. S61–S63). This is the approach we have adopted here.

Intergenerational transmission

Urgency is added to questions of standard of proof by the prospect of intergenerational transformation of neoliberal epidemics, which we introduced briefly in Chapter 1 and revisit here. Communicable diseases are infectious diseases (such as influenza, typhoid and cholera) that are transmitted via contact with infected individuals or pathogens. The prevalence of such diseases in rich countries has fallen considerably since the improvements in sanitation, welfare and health care from the late 19th century onwards (McKeown, 1976). However, they are still very common in some poorer countries: for example, malaria kills 655,000–1.2 million people per year, and tuberculosis an estimated 1.5 million, mainly in the world's poorest countries. These illnesses spread over space. In contrast, non-communicable diseases, which now account for most illness and death in high-income countries, are not contagious and do not spread between individuals. However, the four neoliberal epidemics that we identify in this book (obesity, insecurity, austerity, inequality), while chronic, are simultaneously actually infectious within and between populations as they spread across both space (the transmission of neoliberal ideology across countries with a resulting increase in the burden of ill health) and time – *intergenerational transmission* – whereby the ill-health consequences of neoliberalism are not isolated to the present but seep into the future.

In at least three ways, mechanisms of intergenerational transmission will probably contribute to future adverse health outcomes and rising health inequalities in the high-income world.

The first of these is declining social mobility. Extreme examples include the probable intergenerational effects (operating via loss of economic opportunity for those released from prison, and the effects of their incarceration on families and children) of the epidemic of incarceration in the US, and of youth unemployment rates of 50 per cent or higher in some countries of southern Europe that are now implementing troika-drafted programs of austerity, which simultaneously reduce access to income support and health care. Less extreme examples were explored in Chapter 5. Precarious employment is likely to create a similar trap for the children of those trapped in the 'low-pay, no-pay cycle' (Shildrick et al., 2012b) that is becoming the norm for a substantial proportion of the population in countries where neoliberalism is ascendant. We emphasize, here as elsewhere, that this is a labour market and social policy choice that some governments have made differently. In *The Spirit Level*, although they had comparable data for only eight countries, Wilkinson and Pickett (2010, p. 160) found a dramatic clustering of Norway, Sweden, Finland and Denmark at the low inequality, high social mobility end of the spectrum, with the UK and the US at the high inequality, low mobility extreme. These are pre-recession data, and it is plausible to think that the recession will exacerbate the problem. So much for the neoliberal myth of meritocracy.

The second involves stereotypes – in particular, the individualization of responsibility that blames poverty, worklessness and associated ill health on marginalized individuals and communities themselves, rather than on structural aspects of society and the political choices that shape these. In our earlier discussion of US welfare 'reform', we mentioned the toxic (and racially tinged) alarms about the emergence of an underclass promoted by commentators like Charles Murray. In *Chavs: The Demonization of the Working Class*, British journalist Owen Jones

describes the propagation of images of an idle, loutish and promiscuous working class by mass media and the only slightly less extreme
claims that people get pregnant in order to jump the queue for council (public) housing, have 'a work ethic problem, which is worse than
welfare dependency' or are simply the 'non-aspirational working class'
(a Conservative cabinet minister, a 'senior' Conservative MP and a
Labour Party strategist, respectively, quoted by Jones, 2011, pp. 67, 83,
89). There is, in fact, little evidence to support the idea of cultures of
worklessness; the major issue appears, rather, to be the changing structure of labour markets, and studies have found little evidence of the
stereotypical three generations of worklessness (Shildrick et al., 2012a,
2012b, pp. 125–141), but perhaps that is not the point. Geographer
Tom Slater (2014) has noted similarities between the US discourse and a
Conservative-leaning think tank's effort to promote the idea of 'Broken
Britain' and punitive welfare-to-work programs as a response. Arguably,
this produces a cultural transmission of neoliberal epidemics whereby
existing material disadvantage is reinforced by the continued stigmatization and marginalization, for example in terms of access to employment,
of certain groups and areas, typically working-class or ethnic minority
communities: the 'blemish of place' (Pearce, 2013, pp. 2039–2042; see
also Wacquant, 2007) that makes escape from poverty, high debt, stress
and insecurity especially difficult.

Third, the emerging fields of epigenetics and genetic epidemiology
involve the study of the interactions between genes and the environment whereby some genes are 'turned on' or 'turned off' by the wider
environment in which the host body exists. There is variability within
human genes – some of which is harmless (such as eye colour) and some
of which can lead to a greater risk of particular diseases (such as heart disease or cancer). Epigenetics studies the role of the environment (social,
political, cultural, material) in why these harmful genes are expressed
in some people and populations and not others (G. McCartney, personal communication, 2014). A growing body of evidence indicates that
vulnerability to disease can be transmitted biologically via the interaction between genes and the environment – epigenetics. Genes do
not explain time trends in population health themselves, but via their
interaction with the environment, whereby some people are exposed to
factors that damage genes while others are not. So, for example, some
studies have shown that long-term genetic damage is associated with
deprivation (Hertzman and Boyce, 2010; McGuiness et al., 2012). It has
also been suggested that some of these epigenetic (environmentally produced changes in genes) changes can be inherited and passed between

generations – *biological intergenerational transmission*. However, the most compelling evidence to date for this comes largely from foetal nutritional studies such as the paradigmatic studies of the Dutch famine (Heijmans et al., 2008; Lussana et al., 2008). The Dutch famine (or Hunger Winter) of 1944–1945 was created by a Nazi food blockade whereby rations in the Netherlands fell to between 500 and 1000 calories per day, leading to mass starvation. These studies found that the children of women who experienced the famine had less DNA methylation (gene modification that deactivates the gene) of the maternally imprinted 'insulin-like growth factor II (IGF2)' gene than their younger (non-famine) siblings – six decades later (Heijmansa et al., 2008). This, in turn, was associated with the famine-born children being twice as likely to consume a high-fat diet and have higher rates of obesity (Lussana et al., 2008). The Dutch studies have also found changes in the genes associated with cholesterol, ageing and schizophrenia among the famine babies. So the harmful effects of the neoliberal environment that we now inhabit could cascade down the generations – genetically as well as socially.

No alternatives?

But what if there really is 'no alternative' to neoliberal policies? The assertion that 'there is no alternative' became familiar in the Thatcher era, and similar claims are now made by the political right and even (as noted in Chapter 4) some progressive academics, notably with respect to the need for austerity programs that emphasize expenditure reduction, but also about such issues as the need to maintain labour market flexibility. There are really two separate sets of questions here: one set about policy analysis and the other about hard politics. We deal with issues of policy analysis in this section of the chapter, and present two, somewhat divergent views of the hard politics of fighting neoliberal epidemics in the section that follows.

Returning to the topic of Chapter 2, governments have options in combating the obesity epidemic, although it has to be said that few have used these options effectively. They can start by rejecting the neoliberal rhetoric of individual responsibility, and instead (for example) accept the imperative of avoiding food poverty by ensuring incomes adequate to afford a healthy diet. It is possible, although not easy, to regulate the activities of large transnational corporate marketers of unhealthy food. In New York City, a proposal to prohibit the sale of supersized soft drinks was defeated in the courts after a well-funded campaign by the soft drink industry (Grynbaum, 2012, 2014), but Mexico is actively considering a tax on such drinks, again facing an industry campaign of opposition (Malkin, 2013). Stuckler and colleagues suggest that soft drink consumption did not rise in Venezuela over the past two decades because, unlike Mexico, it does not have a trade agreement with the US that requires it to open its markets to imports and foreign investment (Stuckler et al., 2012b). Planning permissions could, at least in theory, be used to avoid the creation of food deserts, and can certainly be used to make the built environment more activity-friendly (Northridge and Freeman, 2011).

Governments also have a variety of policy instruments with which to address economic insecurity, the topic of Chapter 3. These include both provision of income support and services in kind – the conventional image of the welfare state – and labour market policies such as minimum wage laws and limits on precarious employment. We noted striking differences in the prevalence of low-wage work in high-income countries similarly exposed to globalization and technological change. The effect of public policy under neoliberalism has sometimes been to increase insecurity, whether as a deliberate choice or as collateral damage accepted in the interests of increasing competitiveness, but against the background of such differences it is hard to argue that there is no alternative to the expansion of the precariat.

It is in the context of austerity and inequality – the topics of chapters 4 and 5 – that the range of options available to government becomes clearest. Wherever prescriptions for austerity have been applied post-2008, they have been applied selectively. On the expenditure side, while cutbacks were hitting the poor and vulnerable in the UK, the government was able to commit billions of pounds in future price guarantees in order to convince a foreign firm to build new nuclear power stations – potentially, a tax on power consumers that would flow directly into the firm's treasury (Wintour and Inman, 2013). It was also able to commit £15 billion over five years for a 'roads revolution' that would add 'hundreds of extra lane miles' (Press Association, 2014), while bus fares were rising and routes were being cut as a consequence of cuts to local government budgets (Local Government Association, 2014). The example of soaring prison spending in the US, while income support levels declined and public education expenditure was squeezed (see e.g. Austin et al., 2001, p. 20) in New York, is another striking example.

Claims that expenditure cuts are unavoidable also neglect the revenue side of the equation. Shortly after coming to power, the Conservative-led UK government reduced the marginal income tax rate paid by the highest earners from 50 per cent to 45 per cent. And when revenues are increased under austerity regimes, the impact is sometimes highly regressive. In Greece, cutbacks in social spending, which was already lower than the EU-15 average as a proportion of GDP, were accompanied by tax 'reforms' that meant even some people with incomes below the official poverty line were for the first time subject to income tax, and 'the new tax rates placed a disproportionately heavy burden on low to middle incomes' (Petmesidou, 2013, p. 603). One of us has described the combination of asking hard questions about expenditure priorities with examining both revenue and expenditure sides of the ledger as a strategy of 'interrogating scarcity' (Schrecker, 2013c) – asking why we are so often told that resources are 'scarce' for certain purposes while they seemingly remain abundant for others.

In fact, high-income countries continue to display considerable divergence in how they approach not only labour markets but also questions of taxation, spending and the role of the state. One of the most thoughtful and experienced observers of British social policy pointed out in 2013 that, on then-current projections, by 2017 public expenditure in the UK as a proportion of GDP would be under 40 per cent – lower than any other major market economy, even the US, despite that country's bloated military budget (Taylor-Gooby, 2013). By comparison, Swedish public spending was projected (by the International Monetary Fund) at 46 per cent, and French spending to remain over 50 per cent. A similar observation can be made about revenues: historical data on total tax revenue as a percentage of GDP show major differences over time, and only modest convergence, despite the challenge presented by global tax competition (Streeck and Mertens, 2013). In 2012, total tax revenue as a percentage of GDP was 24.3 per cent in the US, 35.2 per cent in the UK, but 44 per cent or more in Belgium, Denmark, Finland, France, Italy and Sweden (OECD StatExtracts, 2014).

These differences have clear implications for the inequality that was our topic in Chapter 5. We have noted the extreme concentration of wealth in countries like the US and the UK. However, geographer Danny Dorling (2014) has pointed out that similar trends have *not* occurred in many other high-income countries – notably the Scandinavian countries with social democratic welfare regimes, using the classification we introduced in Chapter 1. As he has put it, 'only some rich countries recently set out to become more unequal'. At the other end of the economic distribution, Figure 6.1 shows the proportion of people in selected high-income countries who would have been poor in 2009–2011 (defined as a household income less than or equal to half the

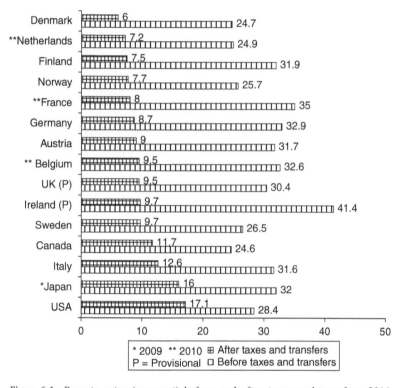

Figure 6.1 Poverty rates (per cent) before and after taxes and transfers, 2011 (unless otherwise noted), in selected OECD countries
Source: OECD Income Distribution database; whole population, poverty ≤ 50% of median income.

median income, after adjustments for household size) based only on their market incomes, that is, if there were no redistribution via taxes and transfers, and the poverty rate after taxes and transfers. This latter rate varies by a factor of three, suggesting that substantial room remains – at least in most of the high-income world – for nationally divergent social policies.

Our vision of a program or policy that would reverse neoliberal epidemics relies on a vision of a re-invigorated welfare state – or, stated another way, a state that is more willing to challenge the values of the unfettered marketplace in order to increase and equalize opportunities for everyone to lead a healthy life. The Finnish social policy unit STAKES described this agenda in terms of redistribution, regulation and (social) rights (Deacon et al., 2005). What are the prospects for such an agenda in the countries where neoliberalization has been most extensive?

Pessimism and optimism about political change

On a pessimistic view, the prospects are dim because of factors in both international and domestic political environments. Schäfer and Streeck (2013, pp. 17–23) argue that the accumulation of government debt over the past decades creates long-term constraints on redistributive social policy. Global tax competition, they say, will seriously limit governments' ability to raise taxes on corporations and high income earners. Vito Tanzi (2008), a former senior official of the IMF, has made this argument more colourfully in terms of the work of 'fiscal termites'. The privatization that Hacker describes as the great risk shift will continue, so the argument runs, under pressure of these fiscal constraints, and will spread to other countries. Meanwhile, governments' continued reliance on financial markets will mean not only that they continue to transfer resources from the tax base as a whole to wealthy bondholders, but also that the shift of power from national governments to 'the markets' over the permissible limits of public policy will be consolidated. 'The markets', and central banks, will exercise a form of solidarity that is inaccessible to citizens, as they have already done through bailouts that subsidized financial speculators, while '[t]he task of national governments... is above all to sell their people on the machinations of international money technocrats and the compromises produced by financial diplomacy' (Schäfer and Streeck, p. 21). There remains, they note drily, the problem of how to sustain growth in the context of continued austerity, and of how to reconcile the demands of democracy with the demands of financial markets. On this view, the post-war settlement between labour and capital in the high-income world is an historical anomaly that is unlikely to persist in an era of globalized production and finance and heavily indebted governments.

These constraints may influence, and be compounded by, domestic political dynamics. One element of these dynamics, which we have already identified, is neoliberalism's tendency to shift public perceptions in the direction of attributing adversity to individuals' own failings, whether these involve the balance of physical activity and diet or the supposed fecklessness and unwillingness to work of the economically marginalized. Veteran Belgian politician Frank Vandenbroucke (1998, p. 47) has pointed out a possible connection between this shift and structural economic change: 'To the extent that skill has become more important as an explanatory factor of quite visible wage inequalities, such inequalities come to have a more "biographical" character: they seem to be more related to personal history and qualifications than to class as traditionally understood.' This shift may contribute to a dynamic identified by Streeck and Mertens (2013, p. 55), who observe that 'the United States could easily solve its fiscal problems by raising its taxes by a few percentage points, to a level that would still remain far short of even the German one', but that the general tendency, not only in the US but also in other countries (including Germany and Sweden), is one of lowering taxes. The continuing retrenchment of public services is likely to intensify 'tax resistance among the well-to-do, who are likely to be unwilling to pay both for the services they buy on their own for themselves and for the publicly funded services they do not use' (Schäfer and Streeck, 2013, p. 18) – the process a former US cabinet secretary referred to as long ago as 1991 as the secession of the successful (Reich, 1991). Thus, neoliberalization tends to be self-reinforcing. As an aside, we wonder whether this process is actually well understood and used strategically by governments. Commenting on the lack of success of New Labour's effort to reduce health inequalities in England between 1997 and 2010, Mackenbach (2010, p. 1249) has observed that 'health inequalities are the result of the cumulative impact of decades of exposure to health risks, some of them intergenerational, of those who live in socioeconomically less advantaged circumstances'. This means that reducing them 'requires a massive re-allocation of societal resources' (p. 1252) and, in his view, 'it is unlikely that a majority of the English electorate would have supported the substantial redistribution of income and wealth that would have been necessary' (p. 1252) to alter the trend of rising health inequalities.

On the brighter side, the Commission on Social Determinants of Health (2008) made 'tackling the inequitable distribution of power, money and resources' one of its three overarching recommendations. And there is no shortage of policies that would accomplish this objective. There is strong evidence that control at work (Bambra, 2011) and community empowerment (Becker, 1999) improve health and well-being. Wealth needs to be redistributed to the communities in which such wealth is actually generated, so that ill health, unemployment or old age does not result in poverty. Social protection systems need to provide a real safety net which protects everyone, perhaps by providing an entitlement to a minimum income sufficient for healthy living (Morris et al., 2007). Security also needs to be increased for those in work – by providing good-quality, secure jobs and ending the spread of zero-hours contracts and casual working. Increasing the rights of trade unions to organize will enable this process from the bottom up. Work also needs to pay, so that in-work poverty, now routine in the neoliberalized world, is a thing of the past. This can be done via the establishment of a living wage (Sonn and Luce, 2008) and does not necessarily require national government action. Local governments and other public agencies can, for example, opt to pay their workers a living wage and to deal only with contractors or suppliers that do the same (Schoenberger, 2000). Over a longer term and on a more ambitious time scale, full employment needs to be reinstated as a core aim of government, so that everyone benefits from any rise in economic growth.

This is, in effect, an effort to replicate the politics of the post-war settlement in Western Europe, which combined an interventionist state with a strong social safety net and a policy of full employment. During that period, life chances were more equal across the population as social mobility increased, health and income inequalities were at their smallest, and the labour movement was actively involved in the democratic process. In the UK, the National Health Service providing free care for all of the population, the welfare state providing a safety net and the nationalization of key industries all occurred in a period of far greater economic uncertainty and debt than that faced in the post-2008 crash. Even now, those rich countries that are the least infected by neoliberalism are those with a stronger social democratic tradition: income inequalities are lower, social mobility is higher and the health of vulnerable groups is better in Sweden than in the UK (Bambra, 2013). In other words, optimists and pessimists agree on the contours of the policies that would roll back neoliberal epidemics, if not about their probability.

Optimists and pessimists appear to find common ground in other areas, as well. One of these is the importance of taking taxation seriously. In 2013 the former clerk of Canada's Privy Council – the head of its federal public service – co-edited a book called *Tax Is Not a Four-Letter Word*, warning that recent tax cuts in that country, notably decreases in national income and sales taxes, had not been preceded by serious public discussion of their implications for what government can do, and for whom. Contributors offered different options for the future, but all agreed on the socially destructive consequences of failing to have a serious conversation about the assumption that a lower-tax future (meaning, in practice, a lower-service future) is always better (Himelfarb and Himelfarb, 2013). Where we live and work, that conversation is not yet happening with respect to a crucial issue: the future funding of the

NHS. While predictions of a £20 billion annual budget shortfall are in the air, few proposals for making good this shortfall through progressive taxation are to be found anywhere in mainstream politics, with user charges widely regarded as inevitable. There is no 'right' level or incidence of taxation, although our preferences are clear, but the conversation needs to start from the recognition that it is simply possible to do more, for more people, with (say) a Swedish or French ratio of government revenue to GDP than with a US one.

Another area of common ground is the importance of democracy. Pessimists whom we have quoted earlier in this chapter concede the precarious prospects for meaningful democracy, as contrasted with what Colin Crouch has called post-democracy, if the available range of economic and social policy options is predetermined by fiscal constraints (Crouch, 2004). For optimists this implies, rather, the urgency of democratic renewal across the rich nations – increasing the power that individuals and communities have over how their society is organized, and who makes political choices on their behalf. For too long, decisions have been made in the name of – but not by – communities and individuals. An electoral choice once every four or five years between two or three geographically and socially remote neoliberal parties is not a healthy democracy. It is, in fact, a bit like going to a supermarket and being offered a choice between one of two or three market baskets with contents picked out by managers with shared dietary preferences. We would add that a precondition for democratic renewal is serious reduction of the role of money in electoral politics – a tall order to be sure, in the wake of the *Citizens United* decision in the US and in a context in which million-pound political contributions are commonplace in the UK.

None of this, it must be emphasized, will be easy; we are not naïve about the scale of the task, but neither are we despondent about the future. In terms of citizen action, we believe that inspiration and hope can be taken from the past achievements of collective action – the trade union gains of the 19th century, the establishment of social democracy in post-war Europe, the civil rights movement of the 1960s US, the feminist revolution of the 1970s, the success of the anti-apartheid struggle in South Africa, and the more recent transnational solidarities that supported the battle to reduce the cost of antiretroviral therapy for HIV. In more current times, there are movements for power to be devolved (such as the Scottish independence movement, which galvanized Scots in advance of the 2014 referendum and may have long-term effects in raising political involvement) and for workers' rights to be extended (Donaldson, 2000; Savage, 2006; Lerner et al., 2008). If serious discussion of how to maintain and protect the NHS has not yet entered the political mainstream, opposition to privatization outside elite circles has been both vocal and widespread. So too, in Europe, has been opposition to the Transatlantic Trade and Investment Partnership (TTIP), which threatens to lock in neoliberalism through investor-state dispute settlement provisions.

At least in the European context, the 'Marmot reviews' of health inequalities in England and in WHO's European Region (Strategic Review, 2010; Marmot and UCL Institute for Health Equity, 2013) have ensured that health inequalities remain on the policy agenda, and Sir Michael Marmot himself has characterized British social policy circa 2013 as 'a grotesque parody of fairness' (Marmot, 2013). At the intergovernmental level, agreements by OECD and G20 governments reached late in 2014 on sharing information on tax avoidance (OECD, 2014) suggest that the view that global tax competition and the damage done by fiscal termites are inevitable may be overstated, although implementation remains uncertain at the time of writing. Inequality is, as we noted in Chapter 5, even on the agenda of the IMF. All these are hopeful signs. We need, as the film maker Ken Loach has argued, to capture the 'Spirit of 1945' and realize that the politics of collectivism and solidarity are our most effective tool in combating ill health and health inequalities. Neoliberal epidemics require a political cure.

Notes

1 Introduction: Politics and Health

1. Full disclosure: One of us (CB) co-wrote a commissioned background paper for this study (Bambra and Beckfield, 2012).
2. Full disclosure: One of us (TS) coordinated one of the nine knowledge networks, on globalization's effects on health, that supported the work of the Commission (see Labonté et al., 2009).
3. In a formal sense, although one can question the voluntariness of labour market transactions in which workers without alternative sources of livelihood are forced to sell their labour power. Given such developments as the rise of 'workfare' programs, this point is of more than academic interest.

2 Obesity: How Politics Makes Us Fat

4. Readers who seek out the obesity prevalence data used to generate these graphs will find country estimates that differ from the ones we have just cited. This is because they were derived using a modelling procedure designed both to standardize for age and to ensure comparability of estimates among a large number of low-, middle- and high-income countries with data of varying quality.

3 Insecurity: How Politics Gets under Our Skin

5. 'Closed shop' means that the employer agrees to hire union members only, or at least that workers must pay union dues in order to remain employed even if they choose not to become members.
6. This said, direct comparison of replacement rates across countries is complicated by substantial variations in the length of time needed to work before qualifying for benefits, the length of time recipients are entitled to benefits, their eligibility (or not) for additional benefits, and the obstacles to benefits to which people are legally entitled.

4 Austerity: How Politics Has Pulled Away Our Safety Net

7. This means that many investments were in complex financial instruments such as derivatives, which make it possible for investors quickly to become liable for losses many times higher than their initial investment.

8. The literature on the origins and consequences of the financial crisis is now too vast even to summarize here. Non-specialist readers are likely to find the accounts of events in 2007–2008 by Johnson and Kwak (2011), *New Yorker* writers James Stewart and John Cassidy (see e.g. Cassidy, 2008; Stewart, 2009) and British commentator John Lanchester (e.g. Lanchester, 2009, 2011) especially useful. Sorkin (2010) provides a riveting account of events in the US, but offers almost too much detail.

9. A reconciliation bill or act is a single piece of legislation that incorporates compromises between versions of a bill passed by the House of Representatives and the Senate.

5 Inequality: How Politics Divides and Rules Us

10. The top marginal rate was later raised to 50 per cent under Labour, then lowered again to 45 per cent by the Conservative-led coalition.

11. More detail on the retreat from national urban policy, without specific reference to drugs or prisons, is provided by Caraley (1992, 1996).

12. This research was conducted as part of a Parliamentary Labour Party inquiry into international health care systems. It is published as Bambra et al. (2014).

13. Level of trust, mental illness, life expectancy, infant mortality, children's educational performance, teenage births, homicides, imprisonment rates, social mobility.

References

Abelson, R. (2009) 'Insured, But Bankrupted by Health Crises.' *New York Times*, July 1.

Albin-Lackey, C. (2014) *Profiting from Probation: America's 'Offender-Funded' Probation Industry* (New York: Human Rights Watch). Retrieved from: http://www.hrw.org/sites/default/files/reports/us0214_ForUpload_0.pdf [accessed 20 November 2014].

Andreyeva, T., Kelly, I.R. and Harris, J.L. (2011) 'Exposure to Food Advertising on Television: Associations with Children's Fast Food and Soft Drink Consumption and Obesity.' *Economics and Human Biology, 9*, 221–233.

Appelbaum, E., Bosch, G., Gautié, J., et al. (2010) 'Introduction and Overview.' In J. Gautié and J. Schmitt (eds.), *Low-Wage Work in the Wealthy World* (New York: Russell Sage Foundation).

Ashton, J.R., Middleton, J. and Lang, T. (2014) 'Open Letter to Prime Minister David Cameron on Food Poverty in the UK.' *The Lancet, 383*, 1631;doi:10.1016/S0140-6736(14)60536-5.

Association of Local Public Health Agencies (2009) *Information Package for Local Public Health Agencies: Put Food in the Budget Campaign* (Toronto: alPHa). Retrieved from: http://www.rrasp-phirn.ca/images/fbfiles/files/CNFB _2009_Information_Package.pdf [accessed 20 November 2014].

Austin, J., Bruce, M., Carroll, L., McCall, P. and Richards, S. (2001) 'The Use of Incarceration in the United States.' *Critical Criminology, 10*, 17–41.

Babb, S. (2005) 'The Social Consequences of Structural Adjustment: Recent Evidence and Current Debates.' *Annual Review of Sociology, 31*, 199–222.

Ball, L., Fuceri, D., Leigh, D. and Loungani, P. (2013) *The Distributional Effects of Fiscal Consolidation*, Working Paper No. 13/151 (Washington, DC: International Monetary Fund). Retrieved from: http://www.imf.org/external/pubs/ft/wp/2013/wp13151.pdf [accessed 20 November 2014].

Bambra, C. (2007) 'Going beyond the Three Worlds of Welfare Capitalism: Regime Theory and Public Health Research.' *Journal of Epidemiology and Community Health, 61*, 1098–1102.

Bambra, C. (2009) 'Welfare State Regimes and the Political Economy of Health.' *Humanity & Society, 33*, 99–117.

Bambra, C. (2011) *Work, Worklessness and the Political Economy of Health* (Oxford: Oxford University Press).

Bambra, C. (2012) 'Social Inequalities in Health: The Nordic Welfare State in a Comparative Context.' In J. Kvist, J. Fritzell, B. Hvinden and O. Kangas (eds.), *Changing Social Equality: The Nordic Welfare Model in the 21st Century* (Bristol: Policy Press).

Bambra, C. (2013) 'In Defence of (Social) Democracy: On Health Inequality and the Welfare State.' *Journal of Epidemiology and Community Health, 67*, 713–714.

Bambra, C. (2014) 'Tackling Health-Related Worklessness: A 'Health First' Approach.' In J. Allen, I. Gilmore, F. Godlee, et al. (eds.), *If You Could Do Just

One Thing...? Nine Local Actions to Reduce Health Inequalities (London: British Academy).

Bambra, C., Barr, B. and Milne, E. (2014) 'North and South: Addressing the English Health Divide.' *Journal of Public Health*, 36, 183–186.

Bambra, C. and Beckfield, J. (2012) *Institutional Arrangements as Candidate Explanations for the US Mortality Disadvantage* (Cambridge, MA: Harvard University). Retrieved from: http://scholar.harvard.edu/files/jbeckfield/files/bambra_and_beckfield_2012.pdf [accessed 20 November 2014].

Bambra, C. and Eikemo, T. (2009) 'Welfare State Regimes, Unemployment and Health: A Comparative Study of the Relationship between Unemployment and Self-Reported Health in 23 European Countries.' *Journal of Epidemiology and Community Health*, 63, 92–98.

Bambra, C., Fox, D. and Scott-Samuel, A. (2005) 'Towards a Politics of Health.' *Health Promotion International*, 20, 187–193.

Bambra, C. and Garthwaite, K. (2014) *Welfare and Austerity*, Report to the Independent Inquiry on Health Equity in the North (Manchester: Centre for Local Economic Strategies).

Bambra, C., Garthwaite, K., Copeland, A. and Barr, B. (in press) 'All in It Together? Health Inequalities, Welfare Austerity and the Great Recession.' In K. Smith, C. Bambra and S. Hill (eds.), *Health Inequalities: Critical Perspectives* (Oxford: Oxford University Press, forthcoming).

Bambra, C., Garthwaite, K. and Hunter, D. (2014) 'All Things Being Equal: Does It Matter for Equity How You Organise and Pay for Health Care? A Review of the International Evidence.' *International Journal of Health Services*, 44, 457–472.

Bambra, C., Netuveli, G. and Eikemo, T. (2010a) 'Welfare State Regime Life Courses: The Development of Western European Welfare State Regimes and Age Related Patterns of Educational Inequalities in Self-Reported Health. Commissioned Paper.' *International Journal of Health Services*, 40, 399–420.

Bambra, C., Pope, D., Swami, V., et al. (2009) 'Gender, Health Inequality and Welfare State Regimes: A Cross-National Study of Thirteen European Countries.' *Journal of Epidemiology and Community Health*, 63, 38–44.

Bambra, C. and Popham, F. (2010) 'Worklessness and Regional Differences in Educational Inequalities in Health: Evidence from the 2001 Census.' *Health and Place*, 16, 1014–1021.

Bambra, C., Smith, K.E., Garthwaite, K., et al. (2010b) 'A Labour of Sisyphus? Public Policy and Health Inequalities Research from the Black and Acheson Reports to the Marmot Review.' *Journal of Epidemiology and Community Health*, 65, 399–406.

Banister, J. and Cook, G. (2011) 'China's Employment and Compensation Costs in Manufacturing through 2008.' *Monthly Labor Review*, 134, 39–52.

Bank of England (2008) *Financial Stability Report* No. 24 (London: Bank of England). Retrieved from: http://www.bankofengland.co.uk/publications/fsr/2008/fsrfull0810.pdf [accessed 20 November 2014].

Bank of England (2009) *Financial Stability Report* No. 25 (London: Bank of England). Retrieved from: http://www.bankofengland.co.uk/publications/fsr/2009/fsrfull0906.pdf [accessed 20 November 2014].

Barr, B., Bambra, C. and Smith, K.E. (forthcoming) 'For the Good of the Cause: Generating Evidence to Inform Social Policies That Reduce Health

Inequalities.' In K.E. Smith, C. Bambra and S. Hill (eds.), *Health Inequalities: Critical Perspectives* (Oxford: Oxford University Press).

Bartley, M. (2004) *Health Inequality: An Introduction to Theories, Concepts and Methods* (Cambridge, MA: Polity Press).

Bartley, M. and Blane, D. (1997) 'Health and the Lifecourse: Why Safety Nets Matter.' *BMJ, 314,* 1194–1196.

Bartley, M. and Plewis, I. (2002) 'Accumulated Labour Market Disadvantage and Limiting Long-Term Illness: Data from the 1971–1991 ONS Longitudinal Study.' *International Journal of Epidemiology, 31,* 336–341.

BBC News (1998) 'Business: The Economy – Governor Tries to Douse North's Fire.' BBC News [On-line]. Retrieved from: http://news.bbc.co.uk/1/hi/business/197995.stm [accessed 20 November 2014].

BBC News (2013) 'Amazon UK Paid £2.4m Tax Last Year, Despite £4bn Sales.' BBC News [On-line]. Retrieved from: http://www.bbc.co.uk/news/business-22549434 [accessed 20 November 2014].

BBC News (2014) ' "Rich List" Counts More Than 100 UK Billionaires.' BBC News [On-line]. Retrieved from: http://www.bbc.co.uk/news/uk-27360032 [accessed 20 November 2014].

BBC TV (2014, February) 'Mind the Gap: London v the Rest' [On-line video]. Retrieved from: http://www.bbc.co.uk/mediacentre/proginfo/2014/09/mind-the-gap-london-vs-the-rest.html [accessed 31 March 2014].

Beatty, C. and Fothergill, S. (2005) 'The Diversion from "Unemployment" to "Sickness" across British Regions and Districts.' *Regional Studies, 39,* 837–854.

Beatty, C. and Fothergill, S. (2014) 'The Local and Regional Impact of the UK's Welfare Reforms.' *Cambridge Journal of Regions, Economy and Society, 7,* 63–79.

Beatty, C., Fothergill, S. and Macmillan, R. (2000) 'A Theory of Employment, Unemployment and Sickness.' *Regional Studies, 34,* 617–630.

Beatty, C., Fothergill, S. and Powell, R. (2007) 'Twenty Years on: Has the Economy of the UK Coalfields Recovered?' *Environment and Planning A, 39,* 1654–1675.

Beaulac, J., Kristjansson, E. and Cummins, S. (2009) 'A Systematic Review of Food Deserts, 1966–2007.' *Preventing Chronic Disease, 6,* A105.

Beaumont, H. (2012) 'Everyday Life's a Challenge in a "Food Desert".' *Halifax Chronicle-Herald* [On-line]. Retrieved from: http://thechronicleherald.ca/thenovascotian/161761-everyday-life-s-a-challenge-in-a-food-desert [accessed 20 November 2014].

Becker, A. (1999) *Perceived Control as a Partial Measure of Empowerment: Conceptualization, Predictors, and Health Effects* (Michigan: University of Michigan).

Beckett, K. and Herbert, S. (2009) *Banished: The New Social Control in Urban America* (New York: Oxford University Press).

Bell, R., Aitsi-Selmi, A. and Marmot, M. (2012) 'Subordination, Stress and Obesity.' In A. Offer, R. Pechey and S. Ulijaszek (eds.), *Insecurity, Inequality and Obesity in Affluent Societies* (Oxford: Oxford University Press for the British Academy).

Bellanger, M.M. and Mossé, P.R. (2005) 'The Search for the Holy Grail: Combining Decentralised Planning and Contracting Mechanisms in the French Health Care System.' *Health Economics, 14,* 119–132.

Benach, J., Amable, M., Muntaner, C. and Benavides, F.G. (2002) 'The Consequences of Flexible Work for Health: Are We Looking at the Right Place?' *Journal of Epidemiology and Community Health, 56,* 405–406.

Benach, J. and Muntaner, C. (2007) 'Precarious Employment and Health: Developing a Research Agenda.' *Journal of Epidemiology and Community Health, 61,* 276–277.

Beynon, H., Hudson, R. and Sadler, D. (1994) *A Place Called Teesside* (Edinburgh: University of Edinburgh Press).

Bird, C.E., Seeman, T., Escarce, J.J., et al. (2010) 'Neighbourhood Socioeconomic Status and Biological "Wear and Tear" in a Nationally Representative Sample of US Adults.' *Journal of Epidemiology and Community Health, 64,* 860–865.

Birn, A.-E., Pillay, L. and Holtz, T.H. (2009) *Textbook of International Health* (3rd ed.) (Oxford: Oxford University Press).

Birrell, I. (2014) 'Obesity: Africa's New Crisis.' *Observer,* September 21.

'Blair Calls for Lifestyle Change' (2006) BBC News [On-line]. Retrieved from: http://news.bbc.co.uk/1/hi/5215548.stm [accessed 20 November 2014].

Blakely, T., et al. (2008) 'Inequalities in Mortality during and after Restructuring of the New Zealand Economy: Repeated Cohort Studies.' *BMJ, 336,* 371–375.

Blanden, J., Gregg, P. and Machin, S. (2005) 'Educational Inequality and Intergenerational Mobility.' In S. Machin and A. Vignoles (eds.), *What's the Good of Education? The Economics of Education in the UK* (Princeton: Princeton University Press).

Bluestone, B. and Harrison, B. (1982) *The Deindustrialization of America* (New York: Basic Books).

Blüher, M. (2010) 'The Distinction of Metabolically 'Healthy' from 'Unhealthy' Obese Individuals.' *Current Opinion in Lipidology, 21,* 38–43.

Bosch, G., Mayhew, K. and Gautié, J. (2010) 'Industrial Relations, Legal Regulations, and Wage Setting.' In J. Gautié and J. Schmitt (eds.), *Low-Wage Work in the Wealthy World* (New York: Russell Sage Foundation).

Bourgois, P. (2003) *In Search of Respect: Selling Crack in El Barrio* (2nd ed.) (New York: Cambridge University Press).

Braithwaite, I., Stewart, A.W., Hancox, R.J., et al. (2013) 'The Worldwide Association between Television Viewing and Obesity in Children and Adolescents: Cross Sectional Study.' *PLoS ONE, 8,* e74263.

Braveman, P.A., Egerter, S.A., Woolf, S.H. and Marks, J.S. (2011) 'When Do We Know Enough to Recommend Action on the Social Determinants of Health?' *American Journal of Preventive Medicine, 40,* S58–S66.

Bray, M.S. and Young, M.E. (2012) 'Chronobiological Effects on Obesity.' *Current Obesity Reports, 1,* 9–15.

Breman, A. and Shelton, C. (2007) 'Structural Adjustment Programs and Health.' In I. Kawachi and S. Wamala (eds.), *Globalisation and Health* (Oxford: Oxford University Press).

Breyer, B. and Voss-Andreae, A. (2013) 'Food Mirages: Geographic and Economic Barriers to Healthful Food Access in Portland, Oregon.' *Health and Place, 24,* 131–139.

Brill, S. (2013) 'Bitter Pill: Why Medical Bills Are Killing Us'. *Time Health and Family.'* [On-line]. Retrieved from: http://healthland.time.com/2013/02/20/bitter-pill-why-medical-bills-are-killing-us/ [accessed 20 November 2014].

Broom, D.H., D'Souza, R.M., Strazdins, L., et al. (2006) 'The Lesser Evil: Bad Jobs or Unemployment? A Survey of Mid-Aged Australians.' *Social Science & Medicine, 63,* 575–586.

Brown, G. (2004) 'Full Text: Brown's Mansion House Speech: Speech Given by the Chancellor at the Mansion House, London.' *Guardian*, June 17.

Brown, W., Deakin, S. and Ryan, P. (1997) 'The Effects of British Industrial Relations Legislation 1979–97.' *National Institute Economic Review, 161*, 69–83.

Brunner, E.J. (1997) 'Socioeconomic Determinants of Health: Stress and the Biology of Inequality.' *BMJ, 314*, 1472–1476.

Bureau of Labor Statistics (2011) Table A-15: Alternative Measures of Labor Underutilization. Bureau of Labor Statistics [On-line]. Retrieved from: http://www.bls.gov/webapps/legacy/cpsatab15.htm [accessed 20 November 2014].

Burke, S., Thomas, S., Barry, S., et al. (2014) 'Indicators of Health System Coverage and Activity in Ireland during the Economic Crisis 2008–2014: From "More with Less" to "Less with Less".' *Health Policy, 117*, 275–278.

Burström, B. (2002) 'Increasing Inequalities in Health Care Utilisation across Income Groups in Sweden during the 1990s?' *Health Policy, 62*, 117–129.

Butland, B., Jebb, S., Kopelman, P., et al. (2007) *Tackling Obesities: Future Choices – Project Report* (London: Government Office for Science). Retrieved from: http://www.foresight.gov.uk/Obesity/Obesity_final/Index.html [accessed 20 November 2014].

Butler, P. (2013a) Food Poverty: 'I was Brought Up Not to Steal. But That's How Bad It's Got.' *Guardian* [On-line]. Retrieved from: http://www.theguardian.com/society/patrick-butler-cuts-blog/2013/jun/24/food-poverty-growth-in-shoplifting-groceries [accessed 20 November 2014].

Butler, P. (2013b) 'Heat or Eat? Or Take Out a Loan, Do Both, and Hope for the Best?' *Guardian*, October 1.

Butler, P. (2014a) 'Atos Contract Comes to an End Bringing Much Relief for Campaigners.' *Guardian*, March 27.

Butler, P. (2014b) 'Bedroom Tax: One in Seven Households "Face Eviction".' *Guardian*, February 12.

Byrne, D. (2005) *Social Exclusion* (Milton Keynes: Open University).

Campbell, N., Willis, K.J., Arthur, G., et al. (2013) 'Federal Government Food Policy Committees and the Financial Interests of the Food Sector.' *Open Medicine, 7*, e107–e111.

Capgemini (2011) *US Metro Wealth Index 2011 Findings* (New York: Capgemini). Retrieved from: http://www.capgemini.com/m/en/doc/2011_US_Metro_City_Wealth_Index_small.pdf.

Caraley, D. (1992) 'Washington Abandons the Cities.' *Political Science Quarterly, 107*, 1–30.

Caraley, D. (1996) 'Dismantling the Federal Safety Net: Fictions versus Realities.' *Political Science Quarterly, 111*, 225–258.

Casals-Casas, C. and Desvergne, B. (2011) 'Endocrine Disruptors: From Endocrine to Metabolic Disruption.' *Annual Review of Physiology, 73*, 135–162.

Cassidy, J. (2008) 'Anatomy of a Meltdown: Ben Bernanke and the Financial Crisis.' *The New Yorker*, December 1.

Chadwick, E. (1843) *Report on the Sanitary Condition of the Labouring Population of Great Britain. A Supplementary Report on the Results of a Special Inquiry into the Practice of Internment in Towns* (London: Clowes & Sons).

Chernomas, R. and Hudson, I. (2013) *To Live and Die in America* (London: Pluto Press).

Chernomas, R. and Hudson, I. (2014) 'To Live and Die in America: Labor in the Time of Cholera and Cancer.' *International Journal of Health Services, 44,* 273–284.

Child Poverty Action Group (2014) 'Child Poverty Facts and Figures' [Online]. Retrieved from: http://www.cpag.org.uk/child-poverty-facts-and-figures [accessed 1 July 2014].

Chopra, M. and Darnton-Hill, I. (2004) 'Tobacco and Obesity Epidemics: Not So Different after All?' *British Medical Journal, 328,* 1558–1560.

Christie, N. (1993) *Crime Control as Industry* (London: Routledge).

Chung, H. and Muntaner, C. (2007) 'Welfare State Matters: A Typological Multilevel Analysis of Wealthy Countries.' *Health Policy, 80,* 328–339.

Citizens Advice Bureau (2013) *Advice Trends: Q3 2012/2013* (London: Citizens Advice Bureau). Retrieved from: http://www.citizensadvice.org.uk//advice _trends_q1_2013-14.pdf [accessed 20 November 2014].

Citizens for Tax Justice (2009) *The Bush Tax Cuts Cost Two and a Half Times as Much as the House Democrats' Health Care Proposal* (Washington, DC: Citizens for Tax Justice). Retrieved from: http://www.ctj.org/pdf/bushtaxcutsvshealthcare .pdf [accessed 20 November 2014].

'City sicker' (2013) *Economist,* October 12.

Clark, S.E., Hawkes, C., Murphy, S.M.E., et al. (2012) 'Exporting Obesity: US Farm and Trade Policy and the Transformation of the Mexican Consumer Food Environment.' *International Journal of Occupational and Environmental Health, 18,* 53–64.

Clark, T. and Heath, A. (2014) *Hard Times: The Divisive Toll of the Economic Slump* (New Haven: Yale University Press).

Clear, T. (2007) *Imprisoning Communities: How Mass Incarceration Makes Disadvantaged Neighbourhoods Worse* (New York: Oxford University Press).

Coburn, D. (2004) 'Beyond the Income Inequality Hypothesis: Class, Neo-Liberalism, and Health Inequalities.' *Social Science & Medicine, 58,* 41–56.

Cohen, D. (2011) 'Will Industry Influence Derail UN Summit?' *British Medical Journal, 343,* d5328.

Cohen, S. and Janicki-Deverts, D. (2012) 'Who's Stressed? Distributions of Psychological Stress in the United States in Probability Samples from 1983, 2006, and 2009.' *Journal of Applied Social Psychology, 42,* 1320–1334.

Collins, B. (2012) *Right to Work Laws: Legislative Background and Empirical Research.* Retrieved from: http://digitalcommons.ilr.cornell.edu/key_workplace/979/ [accessed 20 November 2014].

Commission on Social Determinants of Health (2007) *Achieving Health Equity: From Root Causes to Fair Outcomes. Interim Statement* (Geneva: World Health Organization). Retrieved from: http://www.who.int/social_determinants/ resources/csdh_media/csdh_interim_statement_07.pdf [accessed 20 November 2014].

Commission on Social Determinants of Health (2008) *Closing the Gap in a Generation: Health Equity through Action on the Social Determinants of Health (Final Report)* (Geneva: World Health Organization). Retrieved from: http:// whqlibdoc.who.int/publications/2008/9789241563703_eng.pdf [accessed 20 November 2014].

Cooper, C. (2014) 'International Arms Firm Lockheed Martin in the Frame for £1bn NHS Contract.' *Independent,* November 19.

Cooper, N., Purcell, S. and Jackson, R. (2014) *Below the Breadline: The Relentless Rise of Food Poverty in Britain* (London: Church Action on Poverty, Oxfam and the Trussell Trust). Retrieved from: http://www.trusselltrust.org/resources/documents/foodbank/6323_Below_the_Breadline_web.pdf [accessed 20 November 2014].

Copeland, A., Bambra, C., Nylén, et al. (2015) 'All in It Together? The Effects of Recession on Population Health and Health Inequalities in England and Sweden, 1991 to 2010.' *International Journal of Health Services*, in press.

Cornia, G.A., Jolly, R. and Stewart, F. (eds.) (1987) *Adjustment with a Human Face*, vol.1: *Protecting the Vulnerable and Promoting Growth* (Oxford: Clarendon Press).

Cornwell, T.B., McAlister, A.R. and Polmear-Swendris, N. (2014) 'Children's Knowledge of Packaged and Fast Food Brands and Their BMI. Why the Relationship Matters for Policy Makers.' *Appetite, 81*, 277–283.

Coulter, A., Le Maistre, N. and Henderson, L. (2005) *Patients' Experience of Choosing Where to Undergo Surgical Treatment. Evaluation of the London Patient Choice Scheme* (Oxford: Picker Institute).

Creswell, J., Fink, S. and Cohen, S. (2014) 'Hospital Charges Surge for Common Ailments, Data Shows.' *New York Times*, June 3.

Crouch, C. (2004) *Post-Democracy* (Cambridge, MA: Polity Press).

Cummins, S., Curtis, S., Diez-Roux, A.V. and Macintyre, S. (2007) 'Understanding and Representing "Place" in Health Research: A Relational Approach.' *Social Science & Medicine, 65*, 1825–1838.

Davey, M. (2013) 'Financial Crisis Just a Symptom of Detroit's Woes.' *New York Times*, July 9.

Davis, J. and Tallis, R. (eds.) (2013) *NHS SOS* (London: Oneworld).

Davis, K., Stremikis, K., Squires, D. and Schoen, C. (2014) *Mirror, Mirror on the Wall, 2014 Update: How the U.S. Health Care System Compares Internationally* (New York: Commonwealth Fund). Retrieved from: http://www.commonwealthfund.org/~/media/files/publications/fund-report/2014/jun/1755_davis_mirror_mirror_2014.pdf [accessed 20 November 2014].

Deacon, B., Ilva, M., Koivusalo, M., et al. (2005) *Copenhagen Social Summit Ten Years On: The Need for Effective Social Policies Nationally, Regionally and Globally*, GASPP Policy Briefs No. 6 (Helsinki: Globalism and Social Policy Programme, STAKES).

De Agostini, P., Hills, J. and Sutherland, H. (2014) *Were We Really All in It Together? The Distributional Effects of the UK Coalition Government's Tax-Benefit Policy Changes*, Social Policy in a Cold Climate Working Paper No. 10 (London: Centre for Analysis of Social Exclusion, London School of Economics and Political Science). Retrieved from: http://sticerd.lse.ac.uk/dps/case/spcc/wp10.pdf [accessed 20 November 2014].

Department of Energy and Climate Change (2013) Fuel Poverty [Online]. Retrieved from: https://www.gov.uk/government/uploads/system/uploads/attachment_data/file/226985/fuel_poverty_report_2013.pdf [accessed 11 March 2014].

De Vogli, R., Kouvonen, A., Elovainio, M., et al. (2014a) 'Economic Globalisation, Inequality and Body Mass Index: A Cross-National Analysis of 127 Countries.' *Critical Public Health, 24*, 7–21.

De Vogli, R., Kouvonen, A. and Gimeno, D. (2014b) 'The Influence of Market Deregulation on Fast Food Consumption and Body Mass Index: A Cross-National Time Series Analysis.' *Bulletin of the World Health Organization, 92,* 99–107.

Diderichsen, F., Evans, T. and Whitehead, M. (2001) 'The Social Basis of Disparities in Health.' In M. Whitehead, T. Evans, F. Diderichsen, et al. (eds.), *Challenging Inequities in Health: From Ethics to Action* (New York: Oxford University Press).

Dixon, J.B. (2010) 'The Effect of Obesity on Health Outcomes.' *Molecular and Cellular Endocrinology, 316,* 104–108.

Dobrowolsky, A. (2002) 'Rhetoric versus Reality: The Figure of the Child and New Labour's Strategic "Social Investment State".' *Studies in Political Economy, 69,* 43–73.

Donaldson, G. (2000) 'With Justice for All?' *Fast Company, 38,* 260–270.

Donia Sofio, A., Meneguzzo, M., Mennini, F.S., et al. (2006) *Rapporto CEIS Sanità: Il governo del Sistema sanitario* (Rome: Università degli Studi di Roma Tor Vergata).

Dorling, D. (2009) 'Unemployment and Health: Health Benefits Vary According to the Method of Reducing Unemployment.' *BMJ, 338,* 1087.

Dorling, D. (2014) 'How Only Some Rich Countries Recently Set Out to Become More Unequal.' *Sociologia, Problemas e Práticas, 74,* 9–30.

Dragano, N., Siegrist, J. and Wahrendorf, M. (2011) 'Welfare Regimes, Labour Policies and Workers' Health: A Comparative Study with 9917 Older Employees from 12 European Countries.' *Journal of Epidemiology and Community Health, 65,* 793–799.

Dransfield, S. (2014) *A Tale of Two Britains: Inequality in the UK,* Oxfam Media Briefings (Oxford: Oxfam). Retrieved from: http://oxfamilibrary .openrepository.com/oxfam/bitstream/10546/314152/1/mb-a-tale-of-two -britains-inequality-uk-170314-en.pdf [accessed 20 November 2014].

Drewnowski, A. (2009) 'Obesity, Diets, and Social Inequalities.' *Nutrition Reviews, 67,* S36–S39.

Drewnowski, A. (2012) 'Spatial Analyses of Obesity and Poverty.' In A. Offer, R. Pechey and S. Ulijaszek (eds.), *Insecurity, Inequality and Obesity in Affluent Societies* (Oxford: Oxford University Press for the British Academy).

Drewnowski, A. and Eichelsdoerfer, P. (2010) 'Can Low-Income Americans Afford a Healthy Diet?' *Nutrition Today, 44,* 246–249.

Drucker, E. (2011) *A Plague of Prisons: The Epidemiology of Mass Incarceration in America* (New York: New Press).

Duménil, G. and Lévy, D. (2004) 'Neoliberal Income Trends: Wealth, Class and Ownership in the USA.' *New Left Review, New Series, 30,* 105–133.

Dumont, D.M., Brockmann, B., Dickman, S., et al. (2011) 'Public Health and the Epidemic of Incarceration.' *Annual Review of Public Health, 33,* 325–339.

Dwyer, J. (2009) 'Without Health Care, One Burger from Ruin.' *New York Times,* September 13.

Ehrenreich, B. (2001) *Nickel and Dimed: On (Not) Getting By in America* (New York: Metropolitan/Owl).

Ehrenreich, B. (2009) 'Is It Now a Crime to Be Poor?' *New York Times,* August 8.

Eikemo, T. and Bambra, C. (2008) 'The Welfare State: A Glossary for Public Health.' *Journal of Epidemiology and Community Health, 62,* 3–6.

Emsellem, M. and Mukamal, D.A. (2008) 'The New Challenges of Employment in the Era of Criminal Background Checks.' In A. Bernhardt, H. Boushey, L. Dresser, et al. (eds.), *The Gloves-Off Economy: Workplace Standards at the Bottom of America's Labor Market* (Champaign, IL: Labor and Employment Relations Association).

Esping-Andersen, G. (1990) *The Three Worlds of Welfare Capitalism* (London: Polity).

European Trade Union Institute (2013) *Benchmarking Working Europe 2013* (Brussels: ETUI). Retrieved from: http://www.etui.org/content/download/8852/82473/file/13++Benchmarking+WEB+version+2013.pdf [accessed 20 November 2014].

Eurostat (2014) 'GDP Per Capita in the EU in 2011: Seven Capital Regions among the Ten Most Prosperous.' Eurostat [On-line]. Retrieved from: http://epp.eurostat.ec.europa.eu/cache/ITY_PUBLIC/1-27022014-AP/EN/1-27022014-AP-EN.PDF [accessed 20 November 2014].

Evans, R.G. (1987) 'Public Health Insurance: The Collective Purchase of Individual Care.' *Health Policy, 7*, 115–134.

Evans, R.G. (1997) 'Health Care Reform: Who's Selling the Market, and Why?' *Journal of Public Health, 19*, 45–49.

Evans, R.G. and Stoddart, G.L. (1990) 'Producing Health, Consuming Health Care.' *Social Science and Medicine, 31*, 1347–1363.

Federal Reserve Bank of Chicago (2007) *Intergenerational Economic Mobility in the U.S., 1940 to 2000* (Chicago: Federal Reserve Bank of Chicago).

Feloni, R. (2013) 'Here's How Many Fast Food Ads American Kids See Each Year.' Business Insider [On-line]. Retrieved from: http://www.businessinsider.com/american-children-see-253-mcdonalds-ads-every-year-2013-11 [accessed 20 November 2014].

Ferrie, J.E., Shipley, M.J., Marmot, M.G., et al. (1998) 'An Uncertain Future: The Health Effects of Threats to Employment Security in White-Collar Men and Women.' *American Journal of Public Health, 88*, 1030–1036.

Field, M.G. (2000) 'The Health and Demographic Crisis in Post-Soviet Russia: A Two-Phase Development.' In M.G. Field and J.L. Twigg (eds.), *Russia's Torn Safety Nets: Health and Social Welfare during the Transition* (New York: St. Martin's Press).

Field, M.G., Kotz, D.M. and Bukhman, G. (2000) 'Neoliberal Economic Policy, "State Desertion," and the Russian Health Crisis.' In J.Y. Kim, J.V. Millen, A. Irwin, et al. (eds.), *Dying for Growth: Global Inequality and the Health of the Poor* (Monroe, Maine: Common Courage Press).

Fisher, J.O. and Kral, T.V.E. (2008) 'Super-Size Me: Portion Size Effects on Young Children's Eating.' *Physiology and Behavior, 94*, 39–47.

Fletcher, D. (2007) 'A Culture of Worklessness? Historical Insights from the Manor and Park Areas of Sheffield.' *Policy and Politics, 35*, 65–85.

Food Research and Action Center (2014) [On-line]. Retrieved from: http://frac.org/[accessed 20 November 2014].

Fourcade-Gourinchas, M. and Babb, S.L. (2002) 'The Rebirth of the Liberal Creed: Paths to Neoliberalism in Four Countries.' *American Journal of Sociology, 108*, 533–579.

Frank, J. and Haw, S. (2011) 'Best Practice Guidelines for Monitoring Socioeconomic Inequalities in Health Status: Lessons from Scotland.' *Milbank Quarterly, 89*, 658–693.

Fraser, N. and Gordon, L. (1994) 'A Genealogy of Dependency: Tracing a Keyword of the U.S. Welfare State.' *Signs, 19,* 309–336.

Fraser Institute (2013) *Economic Freedom of the World Annual Report 2013* (Vancouver: Fraser Institute). Retrieved from: http://www.freetheworld.com/release.html [accessed 11 July 2014].

Frederick, C.B., Snellman, K. and Putnam, R.D. (2014) 'Increasing Socioeconomic Disparities in Adolescent Obesity.' *Proceedings of the National Academy of Sciences, 111,* 1338–1342.

Freeman, R.B. (2007) 'The Challenge of the Growing Globalization of Labor Markets to Economic and Social Policy.' In E. Paus (ed.), *Global Capitalism Unbound: Winners and Losers from Offshore Outsourcing* (Houndmills: Palgrave Macmillan).

Freudenberg, N. (2014) *Lethal But Legal: Corporations, Consumption, and Protecting Public Health* (New York: Oxford University Press).

Fröbel, F., Heinrichs, J. and Kreye, O. (1980; orig. German publication 1977) *The New International Division of Labour* (Cambridge, MA: Cambridge University Press).

Fudge, J. and Cossman, B. (2002) 'Introduction: Privatization, Law, and the Challenge to Feminism.' In B. Cossman and J. Fudge (eds.), *Privatization, Law, and the Challenge to Feminism* (Toronto: University of Toronto Press).

Gabbay, M., Taylor, L., Sheppard, L., et al. (2011) 'National Institute for Health and Clinical Excellence (NICE) Guidance on Long Term Sickness and Incapacity.' *British Journal of General Practice, 61,* e118–e124.

Galbraith-Emami, S. and Lobstein, T. (2013) 'The Impact of Initiatives to Limit the Advertising of Food and Beverage Products to Children: A Systematic Review.' *Obesity Reviews, 14,* 960–974.

Gallie, D. (2004) *Resisting Marginalisation: Unemployment Experience and Social Policy in the European Union* (Oxford: Oxford University Press).

Garthwaite, K. (2011) ' "The Language of Shirkers and Scroungers?" Talking about Illness, Disability and Coalition Welfare Reform.' *Disability and Society, 26,* no. 3, 369–372.

Garthwaite, K. (2014) 'Fear of the Brown Envelope: Exploring Welfare Reform with Long-Term Sickness Benefits Recipients.' *Social Policy & Administration, 48,* 782–798.

Gaziano, J. (2010) 'Fifth Phase of the Epidemiologic Transition: The Age of Obesity and Inactivity.' *JAMA, 303,* 275–276.

Gautié, J. and Schmitt, J. (eds.) (2010). *Low-Wage Work in the Wealthy World* (New York: Russell Sage Foundation).

Geronimus, A.T., Hicken, M., Keene, D., et al. (2006) ' "Weathering" and Age Patterns of Allostatic Load Scores among Blacks and Whites in the United States.' *American Journal of Public Health, 96,* 826–833.

Giddens, A. (1998) *The Third Way: The Renewal of Social Democracy* (Cambridge, MA: Polity Press).

Glickman, D., Parker, L., Sim, L., et al. (eds.) (2012) *Accelerating Progress in Obesity Prevention: Solving the Weight of the Nation.* Washington, DC: National Academies Press for the Institute of Medicine.

Goetz, E.G. (1996) 'The US War on Drugs as Urban Policy.' *International Journal of Urban and Regional Research, 20,* 539–549.

Goos, M. and Manning, A. (2007) 'Lousy and Lovely Jobs: The Rising Polarization of Work in Britain.' *Review of Economics and Statistics, 89,* 118–133.

Goran, M.I., Ulijaszek, S.J. and Ventura, E.E. (2013) 'High Fructose Corn Syrup and Diabetes Prevalence: A Global Perspective.' *Global Public Health, 8,* 55–64.

Gordon, D.R. (1994) *The Return of the Dangerous Classes: Drug Prohibition and Policy Politics* (New York: W. W. Norton).

Gortmaker, S.L., Must, A., Sobol, A.M., et al. (1996) 'Television Viewing as a Cause of Increasing Obesity among Children in the United States, 1986–1990.' *Archives of Pediatrics and Adolescent Medicine, 150,* 356–362.

Grossman, G.M. and Rossi-Hansberg, E. (2006) 'The Rise of Offshoring: It's Not Wine for Cloth Anymore.' In *The New Economic Geography: Effects and Policy Implications* (Kansas City: Federal Reserve Bank of Kansas City). Retrieved from: http://www.frbkc.org/Publicat/Sympos/2006/PDF/8GrossmanandRossi -Hansberg.pdf.

Grover, C. and Piggott, L. (2007) 'Social Security, Employment and Incapacity Benefit: A Critical Reflection of a New Deal for Welfare.' *Disability & Society, 22,* 733–746.

Grynbaum, M.M. (2012) 'Soda Industry Maps Strategy to Defeat Bloomberg Plan to Ban Super-Size Drinks.' *New York Times,* June 2.

Grynbaum, M.M. (2014) 'New York's Ban on Big Sodas Is Rejected by Final Court.' *New York Times* [On-line]. Retrieved from: http://www.nytimes. com/2014/06/27/nyregion/city-loses-final-appeal-on-limiting-sales-of-large -sodas.html?module=SearchandmabReward=relbias%3Ar%2C%7B%222%22% 3A%22RI%3A15%22%7D.

Guthrie-Shimizu, S. (2005) 'From Southeast Asia to the American Southeast: Japanese Business Meets the Sun Belt South.' In J.C. Cobb and W. Stueck (eds.), *Globalization and the American South* (Athens: University of Georgia Press).

Gwatkin, D.R., Rutstein, S., Johnson, K., et al. (2007) *Socio-Economic Differences in Health, Nutrition and Population within Developing Countries: An Overview* (Washington, DC: World Bank). Retrieved from: http://go.worldbank.org/ XJK7WKSE40.

Hacker, J.S. (2004) 'Privatizing Risk without Privatizing the Welfare State: The Hidden Politics of Social Policy Retrenchment in the United States.' *American Political Science Review, 98,* 243–260.

Hacker, J. (2008) *The Great Risk Shift* (New York: Oxford University Press).

Hacking, J.M., Muller, S. and Buchan, I.E. (2011) 'Trends in Mortality from 1965 to 2008 across the English North–South Divide: Comparative Observational Study.' *BMJ, 342,* d508.

Halifax Initiative (1999) 'The IMF's Structural Adjustment Programme for Canada 1994–1995.' Halifax Initiative [On-line]. Retrieved from: http://www .halifaxinitiative.org/content/imfs-structural-adjustment-programme-canada -1994-1995-december-1995 [accessed 6 February 2015].

Hamnett, C. (2014) 'Shrinking the Welfare State: The Structure, Geography and Impact of British Government Benefit Cuts.' *Transactions of the Institute of British Geographers, 39,* 490–503.

Hancock, C., Dinsdale, H. and Rutter, H. (2013) *Are Inequalities in Child Obesity Widening? Findings from the National Child Measurement Programme,* Obesity Knowledge and Intelligence (London: Public Health England). Retrieved from: https://www.noo.org.uk/uploads/doc/vid_18988 _PHEconf_Poster_NCMPinequalities_v2.pdf.

Harvey, D. (2005) *A Brief History of Neoliberalism* (Oxford: Oxford University Press).

Hastings, A., Bailey, N., Besemer, K., et al. (2013) *Coping with the Cuts? Local Government and Poorer Communities* (New York: Joseph Rowntree Foundation).

Hatch, E.E., Nelson, J.W., Stahlhut, R.W., et al. (2010) 'Association of Endocrine Disruptors and Obesity: Perspectives from Epidemiological Studies.' *International Journal of Andrology, 33,* 324–332.

Hawkes, C., Chopra, M. and Friel, S. (2009) 'Globalization, Trade, and the Nutrition Transition.' In R. Labonté, T. Schrecker, C. Packer, et al. (eds.), *Globalization and Health: Pathways, Evidence and Policy* (New York: Routledge).

Health and Social Care Information Centre (2014) *Statistics on Obesity, Physical Activity and Diet: England, 2014* (London: HSCIC). Retrieved from: http://www.hscic.gov.uk/catalogue/PUB13648/Obes-phys-acti-diet-eng -2014-rep.pdf [accessed 20 November 2014].

Heijmans, B., Tobia, E., Stein, A., et al. (2008) 'Persistent Epigenetic Differences Associated with Prenatal Exposure to Famine in Humans.' *Proceedings of the National Academy of Sciences, 105,* 17046–17049.

Helleiner, E. (1994) 'Freeing Money: Why Have States Been More Willing to Liberalize Capital Controls Than Trade Barriers?' *Policy Sciences, 27,* 299–318.

Hertzman, C. and Boyce, T. (2010) 'How Experience Gets under the Skin to Create Gradients in Developmental Health.' *Annual Review of Public Health, 31,* 329–347.

Heymann, J. (2006) *Forgotten Families: Ending the Growing Crisis Confronting Children and Working Parents in the Global Economy* (New York: Oxford University Press).

Hilary, J. (2014) 'The Transatlantic Trade and Investment Partnership and UK Healthcare.' *BMJ, 349,* g6552.

Himelfarb, A. and Himelfarb, J. (eds.) (2013). *Tax Is Not a Four-Letter Word* (Waterloo, Ontario: Wilfrid Laurier University Press).

Himmelstein, D.U., Thorne, D., Warren, E., et al. (2009) 'Medical Bankruptcy in the United States, 2007: Results of a National Study.' *The American Journal of Medicine, 122,* 741–746.

Holzmann, R. and Jörgensen, S. (2001) *Social Protection Sector Strategy: From Safety Net to Springboard* (Washington, DC: World Bank). Retrieved from: http://www-wds.worldbank.org/external/default/WDSContentServer/WDSP/ IB/2001/01/26/000094946_01011705303891/Rendered/PDF/multi_page.pdf [accessed 6 February 2015].

Hood, C. (1991) 'A Public Management for All Seasons?' *Public Administration, 69,* 3–19.

Hopkins, S. (2006) 'Economic Stability and Health Status: Evidence from East Asia before and after the 1990s Economic Crisis.' *Health Policy, 75,* 347–357.

Horning, M.L. and Fulkerson, J.A. (2015) 'A Systematic Review on the Affordability of a Healthful Diet for Families in the United States.' *Public Health Nursing, 32,* 68–80.

House of Commons (1991) 'Hansard,' 16 May 1991. Parliament of the United Kingdom [On-line]. Retrieved from: http://www.publications.parliament .uk/pa/cm199091/cmhansrd/1991-05-16/Orals-1.html [accessed 20 November 2014].

Howell, C. (2005) *Trade Unions and the State: The Construction of Industrial Relations Institutions in Britain, 1890–2000* (Princeton: Princeton University Press).

Hudson, R. (2013) 'Thatcherism and Its Geographical Legacies: The New Map of Socio-Spatial Inequality in the Divided Kingdom.' *The Geographical Journal, 179*, 377–381.

Hunter, D.J. (2008) *The Health Debate* (Bristol: Policy Press).

Inman, P. (2013) 'Eurozone Youth Unemployment Reaches Record High of 24.4%.' *Guardian*, November 29.

Institute of Medicine (2012) 'Accelerating Progress in Obesity Prevention: Solving the Weight of the Nation.' National Academies Press [On-line]. Retrieved from: http://www.nap.edu/catalog.php?record_id=13275 [accessed 20 November 2014].

Jaggar, A. (2002) 'Vulnerable Women and Neo-Liberal Globalization: Debt Burdens Undermine Women's Health in the Global South.' *Theoretical Medicine, 23*, 425–440.

Jenson, J. and Saint-Martin, D. (2003) 'New Routes to Social Cohesion? Citizenship and the Social Investment State.' *Canadian Journal of Sociology, 28*, 77–99.

Jessop, B. (1991) 'The Welfare State in Transition from Fordism to Post-Fordism.' In B. Jessop, H. Kastendiek, K. Nielsen, et al. (eds.), *The Politics of Flexibility: Restructuring State and Industry in Britain, Germany and Scandinavia* (Aldershot: Edward Elgar).

Johnson, J.V. and Hall, E.M. (1988) 'Job Strain, Workplace Support and Cardiovascular Disease: A Cross-Sectional Study of a Random Sample of the Swedish Working Population.' *American Journal of Public Health, 78*, 1336–1342.

Johnson, S. and Kwak, J. (2011) *13 Bankers: The Wall Street Takeover and the Next Financial Meltdown* (New York: Vintage).

Jones, A. and Bentham, G. (2009) 'Obesity and the Environment.' In P.G. Kopelman, I.D. Caterson and W.H. Dietz, (eds.), *Clinical Obesity in Adults and Children* (New York: Wiley-Blackwell).

Jones, N.R., Conklin, A.I., Suhrcke, M., et al. (2014) 'The Growing Price Gap between More and Less Healthy Foods: Analysis of a Novel Longitudinal UK Dataset.' *PLoS ONE, 9*, e109343.

Jones, O. (2011) *Chavs: The Demonization of the Working Class* (London: Verso).

Joyce, R. and Sibieta, L. (2013) 'Country Case Study – UK.' In S.P. Jenkins, A. Brandolini, J. Micklewright, et al. (eds.), *The Great Recession and the Distribution of Household Income* (Oxford: Oxford University Press).

Kain, J., Hernández Cordero, S., Pineda, D., et al. (2014) 'Obesity Prevention in Latin America.' *Current Obesity Reports, 3*, 150–155.

Kalleberg, A.L. (2011) *Good Jobs, Bad Jobs: The Rise of Polarized and Precarious Employment Systems in the United States, 1970s to 2000* (New York: Russell Sage Foundation, 2011).

Karanikolos, M., Mladovsky, P., Cylus, J., et al. (2013) 'Financial Crisis, Austerity, and Health in Europe.' *The Lancet, 381*, 1323–1331.

Karasek, R.A. and Theorell, T. (1990) *Healthy Work: Stress, Productivity, and the Reconstruction of Working Life* (New York: Basic Books).

Kaufman, J.S. and Harper, S. (2013) 'Health Equity: Utopian and Scientific.' *Preventive Medicine, 57*, 739–740.

Kawachi, I., Kennedy, B.P., Lochner, K., et al. (1997) 'Social Capital, Income Inequality, and Mortality.' *American Journal of Public Health, 87*, 1491–1498.

Kilpi, F., Webber, L., Musaigner, A., et al. (2014) 'Alarming Predictions for Obesity and Non-Communicable Diseases in the Middle East.' *Public Health Nutrition, 17*, 1078–1086.

King, D. and Wood, S. (1999) 'The Political Economy of Neoliberalism: Britain and the United States in the 1980s.' In H. Kitschelt, P. Lange, G. Marks, et al. (eds.), *Continuity and Change in Contemporary Capitalism* (Cambridge, MA: Cambridge University Press).

Kirk, M.O. (1995) 'When Surviving Just Isn't Enough.' *New York Times*, June 25.

Kollmeyer, C. and Pichler, F. (2013) 'Is Deindustrialization Causing High Unemployment in Affluent Countries? Evidence from 16 OECD Countries, 1970–2003.' *Social Forces, 91*, 785–812.

Kondo, N., Sembajwe, G., Kawachi, I., et al. (2009) 'Income Inequality, Mortality, and Self Rated Health: Meta-Analysis of Multilevel Studies.' *British Medical Journal, 339*, b4471.

Kondo, N., Subramanian, S., Kawachi, I., et al. (2008) 'Economic Recession and Health Inequalities in Japan: Analysis with a National Sample, 1986–2001.' *Journal of Epidemiology and Community Health, 62*, 869–875.

Krieger, N. (2013) 'Ecosocial Theory of Disease Distribution.' YouTube [On-line video]. Retrieved from: http://www.youtube.com/watch?v=5pBnnDJ9HQY.

Krieger, N., Rehkopf, D.H., Chen, J.T., et al. (2008) 'The Fall and Rise of US Inequities in Premature Mortality: 1960–2002.' *PLoS Medicine, 5*, 227–241.

Krippner, G.R. (2011) *Capitalizing on Crisis: The Political Origins of the Rise of Finance* (Cambridge, MA: Harvard University Press).

Kumanyika, S., Jeffery, R.W., Morabia, A., et al. (2002) 'Obesity Prevention: The Case for Action.' *International Journal of Obesity, 26*, 425–436.

Kumanyika, S.K., Rigby, N., Lobstein, T., et al. (2009) 'Obesity: Global Pandemic.' In *Clinical Obesity in Adults and Children* (New York: Wiley-Blackwell).

Lagarde, C. (2014) 'The IMF at 70: Making the Right Choices – Yesterday, Today and Tomorrow (Speech to IMF/World Bank Annual Meeting, Washington, DC).' International Monetary Fund [On-line]. Retrieved from: http://www.imf.org/external/np/speeches/2014/101014.htm [accessed 20 November 2014].

Lambie-Mumford, H. and Dowler, E. (2014) 'Rising Use of "Food Aid" in the United Kingdom.' *British Food Journal, 116*, 1418–1425.

Lanchester, J. (2009) 'It's Finished.' *London Review of Books, 31*, no. 10, 3–13, May 28.

Lanchester, J. (2011) 'The Non-Scenic Route to the Place We're Going Anyway.' *London Review of Books, 33*, no. 17, 3–5, September 8.

Le Grand, J. (2007) *The Other Invisible Hand* (Princeton and London: Princeton University Press).

Leon, D.A., Shkolnikov, V.M. and McKee, M. (2009) 'Alcohol and Russian Mortality: A Continuing Crisis.' *Addiction, 104*, 1630–1636.

Lerner, S., Hurst, J. and Adler, G. (2008) 'Fighting and Winning in the Outsourced Economy: Justice for Janitors at the University of Miami.' In A. Bernhardt, H. Boushey, L. Dresser, et al. (eds.), *The Gloves-Off Economy: Workplace Standards at the Bottom of America's Labor Market* (Champaign, IL: Labor and Employment Relations Association).

Levell, P. and Oldfield, Z. (2011) *The Spending Patterns and Inflation Experience of Low-Income Households over the Past Decade* (London: Institute for Fiscal Studies).

Lever, H. and Huhne, C. (1985) *Debt and Danger: The World Financial Crisis* (London: Penguin).

Leys, C. and Player, S. (2011) *The Plot against the NHS* (Pontypool: Merlin Press).

Lin, J. (2010) 'Parole Revocation in the Era of Mass Incarceration.' *Sociology Compass, 4,* 999–1010.

Local Government Association (2014) 'Funding Needed to Save Vital Concessionary Bus Services.' LGA [On-line]. Retrieved from: http://www.local.gov.uk/media-releases/-/journal_content/56/10180/5971406/NEWS [accessed 20 November 2014].

London Health Observatory (2010) 'Introducing the LHO.' Public Health England [On-line]. Retrieved from: http://www.lho.org.uk/download.aspx?urlid=15463andurlt=1.

London Health Observatory (2012) 'Marmot Indicators for Local Authorities in England, 2012' [On-line]. Retrieved from: http://www.lho.org.uk/LHO_Topics/national_lead_areas/marmot/marmotindicators.aspx? [accessed 5 September 2014].

Lordon, F. (2008) 'Le jour où Wall Street est devenu socialiste.' *Le Monde Diplomatique,* October.

Lundberg, O., Yngwe, M., Kölegård Stjärne, M., et al. (2008) 'The Role of Welfare State Principles and Generosity in Social Policy Programmes for Public Health: An International Comparative Study.' *The Lancet, 372,* 1633–1640.

Lussana, F., Painter, R., Ocke, M., et al. (2008) 'Prenatal Exposure to the Dutch Famine Is Associated with a Preference for Fatty Foods and a More Atherogenic Lipid Profile.' *American Journal of Clinical Nutrition, 88,* 1648–1652.

MacInnes, T., Aldridge, H., Bushe, S., et al. (2013) *Monitoring Poverty and Social Exclusion 2013* (New York: Joseph Rowntree Foundation). Retrieved from: http://www.jrf.org.uk/sites/files/jrf/MPSE2013.pdf [accessed 20 November 2014].

Mackenbach, J.P. (2010) 'Has the English Strategy to Reduce Health Inequalities Failed?' *Social Science and Medicine, 71,* 1249–1253.

Mackenbach, J. and McKee, M. (2013) 'Social Democratic Government and Health Policy in Europe: A Quantitative Analysis.' *International Journal of Health Services, 43,* 389–413.

Madrick, J. (2012) 'The Deliberate Low-Wage, High-Insecurity Economic Model.' *Work and Occupations, 39,* 321–330.

Malik, V.S., Willett, W.C. and Hu, F.B. (2013) 'Global Obesity: Trends, Risk Factors and Policy Implications.' *Nature Reviews Endocrinology, 9,* 13–27.

Malkin, E. (2013) 'Mexico Takes Bloomberg-Like Swing at Soaring Obesity.' *New York Times,* October 16.

Mannion, R. (2005) *Practice-Based Budgeting in the NHS: Lessons from the Past; Prospects for the Future,* Report to the Department of Health (York: Centre for Health Economics, University of York).

Marchak, P. (1991) *The Integrated Circus: The New Right and the Restructuring of Global Markets* (Montreal: McGill-Queen's University Press).

Markusen, A., Hall, P., Campbell, S., et al. (1991) *The Rise of the Gunbelt: The Military Remapping of Industrial America* (New York: Oxford University Press).

Marmot, M. (2000) Inequalities in Health: Causes and Policy Implications. In A. Tarlov and R. St.Peter (eds.), *The Society and Population Health Reader,* vol. 2: *A State and Community Perspective* (New York: New Press).

Marmot, M. (2004) 'Status Syndrome.' *Significance, 1,* 150–154.

Marmot, M. (2013) 'Michael Marmot Speaks at APHA 141st Annual Meeting in Boston (Part 1).' American Public Health Association [On-line video]. Retrieved from: http://www.youtube.com/watch?v=XkCRxWm2duIandlist= PLDjqc55aK3kxfHr649FnW9xih7eeQRErG.

Marmot, M. and Bobak, M. (2000) 'Psychological and Biological Mechanisms behind the Recent Mortality Crisis in Central and Eastern Europe.' In G.A. Cornia and R. Paniccia (eds.), *The Mortality Crisis of Transitional Economies* (Oxford: Oxford University Press).

Marmot, M., Bosma, H., Hemingway, H., et al. (1997) 'Contribution of Job Control and Other Risk Factors to Social Variations in Coronary Heart Disease.' *The Lancet, 350,* 235–240.

Marmot, M., Friel, S., Bell, R., et al. (2008) 'Closing the Gap in a Generation: Health Equity through Action on the Social Determinants of Health.' *The Lancet, 372,* 1661–1669.

Marmot, M. and UCL Institute for Health Equity (2013) *Review of Social Determinants and the Health Divide in the WHO European Region* (Copenhagen: WHO Regional Office for Europe). Retrieved from: http://www.euro.who .int/__data/assets/pdf_file/0004/251878/Review-of-social-determinants-and -the-health-divide-in-the-WHO-European-Region-FINAL-REPORT.pdf?ua=1 [accessed 6 February 2015].

Marmot, M.G. and Sapolsky, R. (2014) 'Of Baboons and Men: Social Circumstances, Biology, and the Social Gradient in Health.' In M. Weinstein and M.A. Lane (eds.), *Sociality, Hierarchy, Health: Comparative Biodemography: Papers from a Workshop* (Washington, DC: National Academies Press).

Martikainen, P., Lahelma, E., Marmot, M., et al. (2004) 'A Comparison of Socioeconomic Differences in Physical Functioning and Perceived Health among Male and Female Employees in Britain, Finland and Japan.' *Social Science & Medicine, 54,* 1287–1295.

Martin, P.M. and Martin-Granel, E. (2006) '2,500-Year Evolution of the Term Epidemic.' *Emerging Infectious Diseases, 12,* 976–980.

Massarelli, N. (2009) 'European Union Labour Force Survey: Annual Results 2008.' *Eurostat: Data in Focus, 3,* 1–8. Retrieved from: http://ec .europa.eu/eurostat/documents/4168041/5945177/KS-QA-09-033-EN.PDF/ 6472d24d-f41a-451f-be48-e11de8cb6d57?version=1.0 [accessed 6 February 2015].

Matthews, S.A., Detwiler, J.E. and Burton, L.M. (2005) 'Geo-Ethnography: Coupling Geographic Information Analysis Techniques with Ethnographic Methods in Urban Research.' *Cartographica: The International Journal for Geographic Information and Geovisualization, 40,* 75–90.

McDonough, P. and Amick, B. (2001) 'The Social Context of Health Selection: A Longitudinal Study of Health and Employment.' *Social Science & Medicine, 53,* 135–145.

McEwen, B.S. (1998) 'Protective and Damaging Effects of Stress Mediators.' *New England Journal of Medicine, 338,* 171–179.

McEwen, B.S. (2012) 'Brain on Stress: How the Social Environment Gets under the Skin.' *Proceedings of the National Academy of Sciences, 109,* 17180–17185.

McEwen, B.S. and Seeman, T. (2009) 'Allostatic Load and Allostasis.' MacArthur Research Network on SES and Health [On-line]. Retrieved from: http://

www.macses.ucsf.edu/research/allostatic/allostatic.php [accessed 20 November 2014].

McGuiness, D., McLynn, L., Johnson, P., et al. (2012) 'Socioeconomic Status Is Associated with Epigenetic Differences in the pSoBid Cohort.' *International Journal of Epidemiology, 14,* 151–160.

McKeown, T. (1976) *The Role of Medicine* (London: Nuffield).

Michaels, D. (2006) 'Manufactured Uncertainty.' *Annals of the New York Academy of Sciences, 1076,* 149–162.

Michaels, D. and Monforton, C. (2005) 'Manufacturing Uncertainty: Contested Science and the Protection of the Public's Health and Environment.' *American Journal of Public Health, 95,* S39–S48.

Milbank, D. (1994) 'Unlike Rest of Europe, Britain Is Creating Jobs, But They Pay Poorly.' *Wall Street Journal,* March 28, A1, A7.

Milberg, W. (2004) 'The Changing Structure of Trade Linked to Global Production Systems: What are the Policy Implications?' *International Labour Review, 143,* 45–90.

Milkman, R. (2008) 'Putting Wages Back into Competition: Deunionization and Degradation in Place-Bound Industries.' In A. Bernhardt, H. Boushey, L. Dresser, et al. (eds.), *The Gloves-Off Economy: Workplace Standards at the Bottom of America's Labor Market* (Champaign, IL: Labor and Employment Relations Association).

Milne, S. (2004) *The Enemy within: Thatcher's Secret War against the Miners* (London: Verso).

Milward, B. (2000) 'What Is Structural Adjustment?' In G. Mohan, E. Brown, B. Milward, et al. (eds.), *Structural Adjustment: Theory, Practice and Impacts* (London: Routledge).

Mishel, L., Bivens, J., Gould, E., et al. (2012) *The State of Working America* (12th ed.) (Ithaca: Cornell University Press).

Moller, H., Haigh, F., Harwood, C., et al. (2013) 'Rising Unemployment and Increasing Spatial Health Inequalities in England: Further Extension of the North–South Divide.' *Journal of Public Health, 35,* 313–321.

Monsivais, P. and Drewnowski, A. (2007) 'The Rising Cost of Low-Energy-Density Foods.' *Journal of the American Dietetic Association, 107,* 2071–2076.

Monsivais, P., Mclain, J. and Drewnowski, A. (2010) 'The Rising Disparity in the Price of Healthful Foods: 2004–2008.' *Food Policy, 35,* 514–520.

Monteiro, C.A., Moubarac, J.C., Cannon, G., et al. (2013) 'Ultra-Processed Products are Becoming Dominant in the Global Food System.' *Obesity Reviews, 14,* 21–28.

Montgomery, S.M., Cook, D.G., Bartley, M., et al. (1999a) 'Unemployment Pre-Dates Symptoms of Depression and Anxiety Resulting in Medical Consultation in Young Men.' *International Journal of Epidemiology, 28,* 95–100.

Montgomery, S.M., Cook, D.G., Bartley, M., et al. (1999b). 'Unemployment, Cigarette Smoking, Alcohol Consumption and Body Weight in Young British Men.' *European Journal of Public Health, 8,* 21–27.

Moodie, R., Stuckler, D., Monteiro, C., et al. (2013) 'Profits and Pandemics: Prevention of Harmful Effects of Tobacco, Alcohol, and Ultra-Processed Food and Drink Industries.' *The Lancet, 381,* 670–679.

Mooney, J., Haw, S. and Frank, J. (2011) *Policy Interventions to Tackle the Obesogenic Environment: Focusing on Adults of Working Age in Scotland* (Edinburgh: Scottish Collaboration for Public Health Research and Policy).

Retrieved from: https://www.scphrp.ac.uk/system/files/publications/policy _interventions_to_tackle_the_obesogenic_environment_0.pdf.

Morris, J.K., Cook, D.G. and Shaper, A.G. (1994) 'Loss of Employment and Mortality.' *BMJ, 308*, 1135–1139.

Morris, J.N., Wilkinson, P., Dangour, A.D., et al. (2007) 'Defining a Minimum Income for Healthy Living (MIHL): Older Age, England.' *International Journal of Epidemiology, 36*, 1300–1307.

Moss, M. (2009) 'The Burger That Shattered Her Life.' *New York Times*, October 4.

Moss, M. (2013) *Salt, Sugar, Fat: How the Food Giants Hooked Us* (London: W.H. Allen).

Muffels, R. and Wilthagen, T. (2013) 'Flexicurity: A New Paradigm for the Analysis of Labor Markets and Policies Challenging the Trade-Off between Flexibility and Security.' *Sociology Compass, 7*, 111–122.

Murray, C. (1984) *Losing Ground: American Social Policy, 1950–1980* (New York: Basic Books).

Narayan, K., Boyle, J.P., Thompson, T.J., et al. (2003) 'Lifetime Risk for Diabetes Mellitus in the United States.' *JAMA, 290*, 1884–1890.

National Center for Health Statistics (2011) *Health, United States, 2010: With Special Feature on Death and Dying* (Hyattsville, MD: US Department of Health and Human Services).

Navarro, V., Borrell, C., Benach, J., et al. (2003) 'The Importance of the Political and the Social in Explaining Mortality Differentials among the Countries of the OECD, 1950–1998.' *International Journal of Health Services, 33*, 419–494.

Navarro, V., Muntaner, C., Borrell, C., et al. (2006) 'Politics and Health Outcomes.' *The Lancet, 368*, 1033–1037.

Newman, K. (2009) 'Post-Industrial Widgets: Capital Flows and the Production of the Urban.' *International Journal of Urban and Regional Research, 33*, 314–331.

Newman, K.S. (1988) *Falling from Grace: The Experience of Downward Mobility in the American Middle Class* (London: Collier Macmillan).

Nickell, S. and Bell, B. (1995) 'The Collapse in Demand for the Unskilled and Unemployment across the OECD.' *Oxford Review of Economic Policy, 11*, 40–62.

Nickell, S. and Quintini, G. (2002) 'The Recent Performance of the UK Labour Market.' *Oxford Review of Economic Policy, 18*, 202–220.

Northern Housing Consortium (2014a) 'Real Life Reform: Monitoring the impact of welfare reform in the North' [On-line]. Retrieved from http://www.northern -consortium.org.uk/reallifereform [accessed 6 February 2015].

Northern Housing Consortium (2014b). *Real Life Reform Report 3* (Sunderland: Northern Housing Consortium). Retrieved from: http://www.northern -consortium.org.uk/assets/Policy%20Documents/RLR%20report%20march% 202014_Layout%201.pdf [accessed 20 November 2014].

Northridge, M. and Freeman, L. (2011) 'Urban Planning and Health Equity.' *Journal of Urban Health, 88*, 582–597.

O'Connor, A. (2014) 'Threat Grows from Liver Illness Tied to Obesity.' *New York Times*, June 14.

O'Dowd, A. (2013) 'Half a Million People Using Food Banks in UK as Food Poverty Grows.' *British Medical Journal, 346*, f3578.

OECD (2009) *Sickness, Disability and Work: Keeping on Track in the Economic Downturn – Background Paper*. Paris: OECD. Retrieved from: http://www.oecd.org/ dataoecd/42/15/42699911.pdf [accessed 5 February 2010].

OECD (2011) *Divided We Stand: Why Inequality Keeps Rising* (Paris: OECD).

OECD (2013) *Health Statistics 2013* (Paris: OECD). Retrieved from: http://dx.doi
.org/10.1787/health-data-en [accessed 15 July 2014].

OECD 'Major New Steps to Boost International Cooperation against Tax
Evasion: Governments Commit to Implement Automatic Exchange of
Information Beginning 2017.' OECD [On-line]. Retrieved from: http://
www.oecd.org/ctp/exchange-of-tax-information/major-new-steps-to-boost
-international-cooperation-against-tax-evasion-governments-commit-to-imple
ment-automatic-exchange-of-information-beginning-2017.htm [accessed 20
November 2014].

OECD StatExtracts (2014) 'Revenue Statistics – Comparative Tables.' Organisation for Economic Co-operation and Development [On-line]. Retrieved
from: http://stats.oecd.org/Index.aspx?DataSetCode=REV. [accessed 20 November 2014].

Offer, A., Pechey, R. and Ulijaszek, S. (2010) 'Obesity under Affluence Varies by
Welfare Regimes: The Effects of Fast Food, Insecurity, and Inequality.' *Economics
and Human Biology, 8*, 297–308.

Offer, A., Pechey, R. and Ulijaszek, S. (2012) 'Obesity under Affluence Varies
by Welfare Regimes.' In A. Offer, R. Pechey and S. Ulijaszek (eds.), *Insecurity,
Inequality and Obesity in Affluent Societies* (Oxford: Oxford University Press for
the British Academy).

Ogden, C.L. and Carroll, M.D. (2010) 'Prevalence of Overweight, Obesity,
and Extreme Obesity among Adults: United States, Trends 1976–1980
through 2007–2008.' National Center for Health Statistics [On-line].
Retrieved from: ftp://ftp.cdc.gov/pub/health_statistics/nchs/Publications/
DVD/DVD_3/Health_E-Stat/obesity_adult_07_08/obesity_adult_07_08.pdf
[accessed 6 February 2015] .

Ogden, C.L., Carroll, M.D., Kit, B.K., et al. (2013) *Prevalence of Obesity among
Adults: United States, 2011–2012*, NCHS Data Brief No. 131 (Hyattsville, MD:
National Center for Health Statistics, Centers for Disease Control and Prevention). Retrieved from: http://www.cdc.gov/nchs/data/databriefs/db131.pdf.
[accessed 20 November 2014]

Ogden, C.L., Carroll, M.D., Kit, B.K., et al. (2014) 'Prevalence of Childhood and
Adult Obesity in the United States, 2011–2012.' *JAMA, 311*, 806–814.

Osborne, D. and Gaebler, T. (1992) *Reinventing Government: How the Entrepreneurial
Spirit is Transforming the Public Sector* (New York: Basic Books).

Östlin, P., Schrecker, T., Sadana, R., et al. (2011) 'Priorities for Research on Equity
and Health: Towards an Equity-Focused Health Research Agenda.' *PLoS Med, 8*,
e1001115.

Ottersen, O.P., Dasgupta, J., Blouin, C., et al. (2014) 'The Political Origins of
Health Inequity: Prospects for Change.' *The Lancet, 383*, 630–667.

Panjwani, C. and Caraher, M. (2014) 'The Public Health Responsibility Deal:
Brokering a Deal for Public Health, But on Whose Terms?' *Health Policy, 114*,
163–173.

Pearce, J. (2013) 'Financial Crisis, Austerity Policies, and Geographical Inequalities in Health.' *Environment and Planning A, 45*, 2030–2045.

Peck, J. and Tickell, A. (2002) 'Neoliberalizing Space.' *Antipode, 34*, 380–404.

Perry, J., Williams, M., Sefton, T., et al. (2014) *Emergency Use Only: Understanding and Reducing the Use of Food Banks in the UK* (London: Child Poverty
Action Group, Church of England, Oxfam GB and The Trussell Trust). Retrieved

from: http://www.cpag.org.uk/sites/default/files/Foodbank%20Report_web.pdf [accessed 20 November 2014].

Petmesidou, M. (2013) 'Is Social Protection in Greece at a Crossroads?' *European Societies, 15*, 597–616.

Pfeffer, F.T., Danziger, S. and Schoeni, R.F. (2013) 'Wealth Disparities before and after the Great Recession.' *The Annals of the American Academy of Political and Social Science, 650*, 98–123.

Pfeiffer, J. and Chapman, R. (2010) 'Anthropological Perspectives on Structural Adjustment and Public Health.' *Annual Review of Anthropology, 39*, 149–165.

Pickett, K.E. and Wilkinson, R.G. (2012) 'Income Inequality and Psychosocial Pathways to Obesity.' In A. Offer, R. Pechey and S. Ulijaszek (eds.), *Insecurity, Inequality and Obesity in Affluent Societies* (Oxford: Oxford University Press for the British Academy).

Piketty, T. (2014) *Capital in the Twenty-First Century* (Cambridge, MA: Belknap Press of Harvard University Press).

Piketty, T. and Saez, E. (2013) 'Top Incomes and the Great Recession: Recent Evolutions and Policy Implications.' *IMF Economic Review, 61*, 456–478.

Pillay, N. (2013) *Report on Austerity Measures and Economic and Social Rights* (Geneva: Office of the High Commissioner for Human Rights). Retrieved from: http://www.ohchr.org/Documents/Issues/Development/RightsCrisis/E-2013 -82_en.pdf [accessed 20 November 2014].

Platt, S. (1986) 'Parasuicide and Unemployment.' *British Journal of Psychiatry, 149*, 401–405.

Pollock, A.M. (2004) *NHS plc: The Privatisation of Our Health Care* (London: Verso).

Popham, F. and Bambra, C. (2010) 'Evidence from the 2001 English Census on the Contribution of Employment Status to the Social Gradient in Self-Rated Health.' *Journal of Epidemiology and Community Health, 64*, 277–280.

Popham, F., Gray, L. and Bambra, C. (2012) 'Employment Status Changes and the Prevalence of Self-Rated Health: Findings from UK Individual Level Repeated Cross-Sectional Data from 1978 to 2004.' *BMJ Open, 2*, e001342.

Popkin, B.M. (2002) 'What Is Unique about the Experience in Lower- and Middle-income Less-Industrialised Countries Compared with the Very-High-income Industrialised Countries? The Shift in Stages of the Nutrition Transition in the Developing World Differs from Past Experiences.' *Public Health Nutrition, 5*, 205–214.

Popkin, B.M. (2007) Global Context of Obesity. In S. Kumanyika and R.C. Brownson (eds.), *Handbook of Obesity Prevention* (Boston: Springer US).

Popkin, B.M. and Slining, M.M. (2013) New dynamics in Global Obesity Facing Low- and Middle-Income Countries. *Obesity Reviews, 14*, 11–20.

Poverty and Social Exclusion (2014a) http://www.poverty.ac.uk/ [accessed 1 July 2014].

Poverty and Social Exclusion (2014b) 'Poverty and Social Exclusion in the UK.' Poverty and Social Exclusion [On-line]. Retrieved from: http://www.poverty.ac .uk/sites/default/files/attachments/17Jun14%20Poverty%20in%20the%20UK %20press%20release_PSE%20conference.pdf [accessed 20 November 2014].

Press Association (2014) 'Cameron to Announce £15bn Plan to Improve UK's 100 Road Blackspots.' *Guardian*, November 10.

Prince, M.J. (1999) 'From Health and Welfare to Stealth and Farewell: Federal Social Policy, 1980–2000.' In L.A. Pal (ed.), *How Ottawa Spends, 1999–2000 –*

Shape Shifting: Canadian Governance Toward the 21st Century (Toronto: Oxford University Press).

Przeworski, A., Bardhan, P., Bresser Pereira, L.C., et al. (1995) *Sustainable Democracy* (Cambridge, MA: Cambridge University Press).

Public Health England (2013) *Longer Lives* [On-line]. Retrieved from: http://longerlives.phe.org.uk/ [accessed 31 March 2014].

Public Health England (2014) *Stockton-on-Tees Unitary Authority: Health Profile 2014* (London: Public Health England).

Quinlan, M. and Bohle, P. (2009) 'Overstretched and Unreciprocated Commitment: Reviewing Research on the Occupational Health and Safety Effects of Downsizing and Job Insecurity.' *International Journal of Health Services, 39*, 1–44.

Quinlan, M., Mayhew, C. and Bohle, P. (2001) 'The Global Expansion of Precarious Employment, Work Disorganization, and Consequences for Occupational Health: A Review of Recent Research.' *International Journal of Health Services, 31*, 335–414.

Ramesh, R. (2013) 'Atos Benefit Claimants Face Biased Medical Assessments, Doctor Alleges.' *Guardian*, May 16.

RealtyTrac (2014) U.S. Foreclosure Activity Decreases 10 Percent in February from January Jump to Lowest Level in More Than 7 Years. RealtyTrac [On-line]. Retrieved from: http://www.realtytrac.com/content/foreclosure-market-report/realtytrac-february-2014-us-foreclosure-market-report-7997 [accessed 20 November 2014].

Reich, R. (1991) 'Secession of the Successful.' *New York Times Magazine*, January 20, 16–17, 42–45.

Rennie, K.L. and Jebb, S.A. (2005) 'Prevalence of Obesity in Great Britain.' *Obesity Reviews, 6*, 11–12.

Reynolds, L., Lister, J., Scott-Samuel, A., et al. (2011) 'Liberating the NHS: Source and Destination of the Lansley Reform.' University of Liverpool [On-line]. Retrieved from: http://pcwww.liv.ac.uk/~alexss/toryattackonnhs.pdf [accessed 20 November 2014].

Reynolds, L.A. (2011) 'Two Issues with Competition in Healthcare.' *BMJ, 343*, d4735.

Reynolds, T. (2010) 'Dispatches from the Emergency Room.' *New Left Review, New Series, 61*, 49–57.

Ridzi, F. and London, A.S. (2006) ' "It's Great When People Don't Even Have Their Welfare Cases Opened": TANF Diversion as Process and Lesson.' *Review of Policy Research, 23*, 725–743.

Rolnik, R. (2013) *Report of the Special Rapporteur on Adequate Housing as a Component of the Right to an Adequate Standard of Living, and on the Right to Non-Discrimination in this Context: Mission to the United Kingdom of Great Britain and Northern Ireland* No. A/HRC/25/54/Add.2 (New York: United Nations). Retrieved from: http://www.ohchr.org/EN/HRBodies/HRC/RegularSessions/Session25/Documents/A_HRC_25_54_Add.2_ENG.DOC [accessed 20 November 2014].

Rosenthal, E. (2014) 'As Insurers Try to Limit Costs, Providers Hit Patients with More Separate Fees.' *New York Times*, October 26.

Ross, A. (ed.) (1997) *No Sweat: Fashion, Free Trade, and the Rights of Garment Workers* (London: Verso).

Ross, N., Wolfson, M., Kaplan, G., et al. (2005a) 'Income Inequality as a Determinant of Health.' In J. Heymann, C. Hertzman, M.L. Barer, et al. (eds.), *Healthier Societies: From Analysis to Action* (New York: Oxford University Press).

Ross, N.A., Dorling, D., Dunn, J.R., et al. (2005b) 'Metropolitan Income Inequality and Working-Age Mortality: A Cross-Sectional Analysis Using Comparable Data from Five Countries.' *Journal of Urban Health, 82*, 101–110.

Ruan, N. and Reichman, N. (2014) *Scheduling Shortfalls: Hours Parity as the New Pay Equity*, Legal Research Paper Series Working Paper No. 14–02 (Denver: University of Denver Sturm College of Law). Retrieved from: http://papers.ssrn.com/sol3/papers.cfm?abstract_id=2337245## [accessed 20 November 2014].

Rudas, N., Tondo, L., Musio, A., et al. (1991) 'Unemployment and Depression: Results of a Psychometric Evaluation.' *Minerva Psichiatr, 32*, 205–209.

Russell, D. (2004) *Looking North: Northern England and the National Imagination* (Manchester: Manchester University Press).

Rydin, Y., Bleahu, A., Davies, M., et al. (2012) 'Shaping Cities for Health: Complexity and the Planning of Urban Environments in the 21st Century.' *The Lancet, 379*, 2079–2108.

Saez, E. and Zucman, G. (2014) *Wealth Inequality in the United States since 1913: Evidence from Capitalized Income Tax Data*, NBER Working Paper No. 20625 (Cambridge, MA: National Bureau of Economic Research). Retrieved from: http://gabriel-zucman.eu/files/SaezZucman2014.pdf [accessed 20 November 2014].

Sassen, S. (2001) *The Global City: New York, London, Tokyo* (2nd ed.) (Princeton: Princeton University Press).

Sassen, S. (2002) 'Deconstructing Labor Demand in Today's Advanced Economies: Implications for Low-wage Employment.' In F. Munger (ed.), *Laboring below the Line: The New Ethnography of Poverty, Low-wage Work and Survival in the Global Economy* (New York: Russell Sage Foundation).

Sassen, S. (2009) 'When Local Housing Becomes an Electronic Instrument: The Global Circulation of Mortgages – A Research Note.' *International Journal of Urban and Regional Research, 33*, 411–426.

Sassen, S. (2011) 'Beyond Social Exclusion: New Logics of Expulsion.' In 6th Annual Research Conference on Homelessness in Europe: Homelessness, Migration and Demographic Change in Europe, Pisa, Italy [On-line video]. Retrieved from: http://www.dailymotion.com/video/xl7upb_saskia-sassen-logics-of-expulsion-a-savage-sorting-of-winners-and-losers_news [accessed 20 November 2014].

Savage, L. (2006) 'Justice for Janitors: Scales of Organizing and Representing Workers.' *Antipode, 38*, 645–666.

Schäfer, A. and Streeck, W. (2013) 'Introduction: Politics in the Age of Austerity.' In A. Schäfer and W. Streeck (eds.), *Politics in the Age of Austerity* (Cambridge, MA: Polity Press).

Scharpf, F. (2013) 'Monetary Union, Fiscal Crisis and the Disabling of Democratic Accountability.' In A. Schäfer and W. Streeck (eds.), *Politics in the Age of Austerity* (Cambridge, MA: Polity Press).

Schleiter, M.K. and Statham, A. (2002) 'U.S. Welfare Reform and Structural Adjustment Policies.' *Anthropological Quarterly, 75*, 759–764.

Schneiderman, D. (2008) *Constitutionalizing Economic Globalization: Investment Rules and Democracy's Promise* (Cambridge, MA: Cambridge University Press).

Schoenberger, E. (2000) 'The Living Wage in Baltimore: Impacts and Reflections.' *Review of Radical Political Economics, 32*, 428–436.

Schrecker, T. (2013a) 'Beyond "Run, Knit and Relax": Can Health Promotion in Canada Advance the Social Determinants of Health Agenda?' *Healthcare Policy, 9*, suppl., 48–58.

Schrecker, T. (2013b) 'Can Health Equity Survive Epidemiology? Standards of Proof and Social Determinants of Health.' *Preventive Medicine, 57*, 741–744.

Schrecker, T. (2013c) 'Interrogating Scarcity: How to Think about "Resource-Scarce Settings".' *Health Policy and Planning, 28*, 400–409.

Schrecker, T., Barten, F. and Mohindra, K.S. (2012) 'Metropolitan Health in a Globalizing World.' In T. Schrecker (ed.), *Ashgate Research Companion to the Globalization of Health* (Farnham, Surrey: Ashgate).

Schrecker, T., Chapman, A., Labonté, R., et al. (2010) 'Advancing Health Equity in the Global Marketplace: How Human Rights Can Help.' *Social Science and Medicine, 71*, 1520–1526.

Schuring, M., Burdorf, A., Voorham, A., et al. (2009) 'Effectiveness of a Health Promotion Programme for Long-Term Unemployed Subjects with Health Problems: A Randomised Controlled Trial.' *Journal of Epidemiology and Community Health, 63*, 893–899.

Scott-Samuel, A., Bambra, C., Collins, C., et al. (2014) The Impact of Thatcherism on Health and Wellbeing in Britain, *International Journal of Health Services, 44*, 53–72.

Scruggs, L. and Allan, J. (2006) 'Welfare State Decommodification in Eighteen OECD Countries: A Replication and Revision.' *Journal of European Social Policy, 16*, 55–72.

Scruggs, L., Detlef, J. and Kuitto, K. (2014) *Comparative Welfare Entitlements Dataset 2*, Version 2014–03 (Connecticut: University of Connecticut & University of Greifswald) [On-line]. Retrieved from: http://cwed2.org/ [accessed 20 November 2014].

Seabrook, J. (2013) 'Pauper Management by G4S, Serco and Atos Is Inspired by a Punitive Past.' *Guardian*, November 25.

Seccombe, K. (2009) 'Life after Welfare Reform.' In C.A. Broussard and A.L. Joseph (eds.), *Family Poverty in Diverse Contexts* (New York: Routledge).

Sekine, M., Chandola, T., Martikainen, P., et al. (2009) 'Socioeconomic Inequalities in Physical and Mental Functioning of British, Finnish, and Japanese Civil Servants: Role of Job Demand, Control, and Work Hours.' *Social Science & Medicine, 69*, 1417–1425.

Seymour, R. (2014) 'Zero-Hours Contracts, and the Sharp Whip of Insecurity That Controls Us All.' *Guardian*.

Shaw, C., Blakeley, T., Atkinson, J. (2005) 'Do Social and Economic Reforms Change Socioeconomic Inequalities in Child Mortality? A Case Study: New Zealand 1981–1999.' *Journal of Epidemiology and Community Health, 59*, 638–644.

Sherman, S. (1993) 'How Will We Live with the Tumult?' *Fortune, 128*, 123–125.

Shields, J. and Evans, B.M. (1998) *Shrinking the State: Globalization and Public Administration 'Reform'* (Halifax: Fernwood Publishing).

Shih, M., Dumke, K.A., Goran, M.I., et al. (2013) 'The Association between Community-Level Economic Hardship and Childhood Obesity Prevalence in Los Angeles.' *Pediatric Obesity, 8*, 411–417.

Shildrick, T., MacDonald, R., Furlong, A., et al. (2012a) *Are 'Cultures of Worklessness' Passed Down the Generations?* (London: Joseph Rowntree Foundation). Retrieved from: http://www.jrf.org.uk/sites/files/jrf/worklessness-families-employment-full.pdf [accessed 20 November 2014].

Shildrick, T., MacDonald, R., Webster, C., et al. (2012b) *Poverty and Insecurity: Life in Low-pay, No-pay Britain* (Bristol: Policy Press).

Shkolnikov, V.M., Andreev, E.M., Leon, D.A., et al. (2004) 'Mortality Reversal in Russia: The Story So Far.' *Hygiea Internationalis, 4*, 29–80.

Slater, T. (2014) 'The Myth of 'Broken Britain': Welfare Reform and the Production of Ignorance.' *Antipode, 46*, 948–969.

Smyth, C., Sylvester, R. and Thomson, A. (2014) 'NHS Reforms Our Worst Mistake, Tories Admit.' *The Times*, October 13.

Social Mobility and Child Poverty Commission (2014) *Elitist Britain* (London: Social Mobility and Child Poverty Commission).

Somers, M. (2008) *Genealogies of Citizenship: Markets, Statelessness, and the Right to Have Rights* (Cambridge, MA: Cambridge University Press).

Sonn, P.K. and Luce, S. (2008) 'New Directions for the Living Wage Movement.' In A. Bernhardt, H. Boushey, L. Dresser, et al. (eds.), *The Gloves-Off Economy: Workplace Standards at the Bottom of America's Labor Market* (Champaign, IL: Labor and Employment Relations Association).

Sorkin, A.R. (2010) *Too Big to Fail* (revised ed.) (New York: Penguin).

Special Interest Group of Municipal Authorities (outside London) within the LGA (2013) *A Fair Future? The True Impact of Funding Reductions on Local Government* (Barnsley: SIGOMA). Retrieved from: http://www.sigoma.gov.uk/ Docs/sigomareports/A%20Fair%20Future%202013.pdf [accessed 20 November 2014].

Standing, G. (2014) *The Precariat: The New Dangerous Class* (revised ed.) (London: Bloomsbury).

Stevens, G., Singh, G., Lu, Y., et al. (2012) 'National, Regional, and Global Trends in Adult Overweight and Obesity Prevalences.' *Population Health Metrics, 10*, 22.

Stevenson, R.W. (1995) 'Smitten by Britain, Business Rushes In.' *New York Times*, October 15.

Stewart, J.B. (2009) 'Eight Days: The Battle to Save the American Financial System.' *The New Yorker*, September 21, 58–81.

Strategic Review of Health Inequalities in England post-2010 (2010) *Fair Society, Healthy Lives: The Marmot Review* (London: The Marmot Review). Retrieved from: http://www.instituteofhealthequity.org/projects/fair-society-healthy -lives-the-marmot-review/fair-society-healthy-lives-full-report [accessed 6 February 2015].

Streeck, W. and Mertens, D. (2013) 'Public Finance and the Decline of State Capacity in Democratic Capitalism.' In A. Schäfer and W. Streeck (eds.), *Politics in the Age of Austerity* (Cambridge, MA: Polity Press).

Stuckler, D. and Basu, S. (2013) *The Body Economic: Why Austerity Kills* (London: Allan Lane).

Stuckler, D., Basu, S. and McKee, M. (2011) 'Commentary: UN High Level Meeting on Non-Communicable Diseases: An Opportunity for Whom?' *British Medical Journal, 343*, d5336.

Stuckler, D., King, L. and McKee, M. (2012a) 'The Disappearing Health Effects of Rapid Privatisation: A Case of Statistical Obscurantism?' *Social Science and Medicine, 75*, 23–31.

Stuckler, D., McKee, M., Ebrahim, S., et al. (2012b) 'Manufacturing Epidemics: The Role of Global Producers in Increased Consumption of Unhealthy Commodities Including Processed Foods, Alcohol, and Tobacco.' *PLoS Med, 9*, e1001235.

Swarns, R.L. (2014) 'For a Worker with Little Time between 3 Jobs, a Nap Has Fatal Consequences.' *New York Times*, September 29.

Syal, R. (2014) 'Benefit Mismanagement Hurting Sick and Disabled, Watchdog Says.' *Guardian*, February 27.

Tanzi, V. (2008) 'The Role of the State and Public Finance in the Next Generation.' *OECD Journal on Budgeting, 8*, 1–27.

Tarasuk, V., Dachner, N. and Loopstra, R. (2014) 'Food Banks, Welfare, and Food Insecurity in Canada.' *British Food Journal, 116*, 1405–1417.

Tarlov, A. (1996) 'Social Determinants of Health: The Sociobiological Translation.' In D. Blane, E. Brunner and R. Wilkinson (eds.), *Health and Social Organization: Towards a Health Policy for the 21st Century* (London UK: Routledge).

Taubes, G. and Couzens, C.K. (2012) 'Big Sugar's Sweet Little Lies.' *Mother Jones*, November/December. Retrieved from: http://www.motherjones.com/environment/2012/10/sugar-industry-lies-campaign. [accessed 20 November 2014].

Taylor-Gooby, P. (2008) 'The New Welfare State Settlement in Europe.' *European Societies, 10*, 3–24.

Taylor-Gooby, P. (2013) 'UK Heading for Bottom Place on Public Spending.' Poverty and Social Exclusion [On-line]. Retrieved from: http://www.poverty .ac.uk/articles-government-cuts-international-comparisons-public-spending-whats-new/uk-heading-bottom-place. [accessed 20 November 2014]

Taylor-Robinson, D., Rougeaux, E., Harrison, D., et al. (2013) 'The Rise of Food Poverty in the UK.' *BMJ, 347*, f7157.

Thomas, B., Dorling, D. and Smith, G.D. (2010) 'Inequalities in Premature Mortality in Britain: Observational Study from 1921 to 2007.' *BMJ, 341*, c3639.

Thompson, J. and Smeeding, T.M. (2013) 'Country Case Study – USA.' In S.P. Jenkins, A. Brandolini, J. Micklewright, et al. (eds.), *The Great Recession and the Distribution of Household Income* (Oxford: Oxford University Press).

Thow, A.M. and Hawkes, C. (2009) 'The Implications of Trade Liberalization for Diet and Health: A Case Study from Central America.' *Globalization and Health, 5*, 5.

Thow, A.M., Snowdon, W., Labonté, R., et al. (2014) 'Will the Next Generation of Preferential Trade and Investment Agreements Undermine Prevention of Noncommunicable Diseases? A Prospective Policy Analysis of the Trans Pacific Partnership Agreement.' *Health Policy*, doi: 10.1016/j.healthpol.2014.08.002.

Tickell, A. and Peck, J. (2003) 'Making Global Rules: Globalization or Neoliberalization?' In J. Peck and H. Wai-chung Yeung (eds.), *Remaking the Global Economy: Economic and Geographical Perspectives* (London: Sage).

Tirado, L. (2014) ' "Poor People Don't Plan Long-Term. We'll Just Get Our Hearts Broken".' *Observer*. Retrieved from: http://www.theguardian.com/society/2014/sep/21/linda-tirado-poverty-hand-to-mouth-extract [accessed 20 November 2014].

Tourigny, S.C. (2001) 'Some New Killing Trick: Welfare Reform and Drug Markets in a US Urban Ghetto.' *Social Justice, 28,* 49–71.

Townsend, P., Davidson, N. and Whitehead, M. (eds.) (1992) *Inequalities in Health: The Black Report and The Health Divide* (London: Penguin).

Toynbee, P. (2003) *Hard Work: Life in Low-Pay Britain* (London: Bloomsbury).

Travis, J., Western, B. and Redburn, S. (eds.) (2014). *The Growth of Incarceration in the United States: Exploring Causes and Consequences – Report of the Committee on Causes and Consequences of High Rates of Incarceration, Committee on Law and Justice, Division of Behavioral and Social Sciences and Education* (Washington, DC: National Academies Press).

Tremblay, M.S. and Willms, J.D. (2003) 'Is the Canadian Childhood Obesity Epidemic Related to Physical Inactivity?' *International Journal of Obesity, 27,* 1100–1105.

Treuhaft, S. and Karpyn, A. (2010) *The Grocery Gap: Who Has Access to Healthy Food and Why It Matters* (Oakland, CA: PolicyLink). Retrieved from: http://community-wealth.org/sites/clone.community-wealth.org/files/downloads/report-treuhaft-karpyn.pdf. [accessed 6 February 2015].

Uberti, D. (2014) 'The Death of a Great American City: Why Does Anyone Still Live in Detroit?' *Guardian,* April 3.

Uchitelle, L., Kleinfeld, N.R., Bragg, R., et al. (1996) *The Downsizing of America* (New York: Times Books).

United Nations Human Settlements Programme (UN-HABITAT) (2008) *State of the World's Cities 2010/2011 – Cities for All: Bridging the Urban Divide* (London: Earthscan). Retrieved from: http://mirror.unhabitat.org/pmss/getElectronicVersion.aspx?nr=2917&alt=1 [accessed 6 February 2015].

US Bureau of Labor Statistics (2013) 'Coal Fatalities for 1900 through 2013' [On-line]. Retrieved from: http://www.msha.gov/stats/centurystats/coalstats.asp [accessed 5 September 2014].

Useem, M. (1996) *Investor Capitalism: How Money Managers are Changing the Face of Corporate America* (New York: Basic Books).

US House of Representatives (1997) *Conduct of Monetary Policy: Report of the Federal Reserve Board, Hearing before the Subcommittee on Domestic and International Monetary Policy, Committee on Banking and Financial Services* No. 105–6 (Washington, DC: US Government Printing Office).

Valkonen, T., Martikainen, P., Jalovaara, M., et al. (2000) 'Changes in Socioeconomic Inequalities in Mortality during an Economic Boom and Recession among Middle-aged Men and Women in Finland.' *European Journal of Public Health, 10,* 274–80.

Van Cauter, E. and Spiegel, K. (1999) 'Sleep as a Mediator of the Relationship between Socioeconomic Status and Health: A Hypothesis.' *Annals of the New York Academy of Sciences, 896,* 254–261.

van Der Wel, K., Dahl, E. and Thielen, K (2012) 'Social Inequalities in "sickness": Does Welfare State Regime Type Make a Difference? A Multilevel Analysis of Men and Women in 26 European Countries.' *International Journal of Health Services, 42,* 235–255.

Vandenbroeck, P., Goossens, J. and Clemens, M. (2007a) *Tackling Obesities: Future Choices – Building the Obesity System Map* (London: Government Office for Science). Retrieved from: http://www.foresight.gov.uk/Obesity/12.pdf [accessed 20 November 2014].

Vandenbroeck, P., Goossens, J. and Clemens, M. (2007b) *Tackling Obesities: Future Choices – Obesity System Atlas* (London: Government Office for Science). Retrieved from: http://www.foresight.gov.uk/Obesity/11.pdf [accessed 20 November 2014].

Vandenbroucke, F. (1998) *Globalisation, Inequality and Social Democracy* (London: Institute for Public Policy Research).

Velkoff, V. (2014) 'Income, Poverty, and Health Insurance Coverage: 2013.' United States Census Bureau, US Department of Commerce [Online]. Retrieved from: http://www.census.gov/content/dam/Census/newsroom/press-kits/2014/20140916_ip_slides_plot_points.pdf [accessed 20 November 2014].

Virtanen, P., Vahtera, J., Kivimäki, M., et al. (2002) 'Employment Security and Health.' *Journal of Epidemiology and Community Health, 56*, 569–574.

Wacquant, L. (2004) *Punir les pauvres: Le nouveau gouvernement de l'insecurité sociale* (Paris: Agone).

Wacquant, L. (2007) 'Territorial Stigmatization in the Age of Advanced Marginality.' *Thesis Eleven, 91*, 66–77.

Wacquant, L. (2009) *Punishing the Poor: The Neoliberal Government of Social Insecurity* (Durham: Duke University Press).

Wallace, R. and Wallace, D. (1998) *A Plague on Your Houses: How New York Was Burned Down and National Public Health Crumbled* (London: Verso).

Wallace, R. and Wallace, D.N. (2005) 'Structured Psychosocial Stress and the US Obesity Epidemic.' *Journal of Biological Systems, 13*, 363–384.

Walsh, D., Taulbut, M. and Hanlon, P. (2010) 'The Aftershock of Deindustrialization: Trends in Mortality in Scotland and Other Parts of Post-Industrial Europe.' *The European Journal of Public Health, 20*, 58–64.

Ward, K. and England, K. (2007) 'Introduction: Reading Neoliberalization.' In K. England and K. Ward (eds.), *Neoliberalization: States, Networks, People* (Oxford: Blackwell).

Warren, E. (2007) 'The Vanishing Middle Class.' In J. Edwards, M. Crain and A.L. Kalleberg (eds.), *Ending Poverty in America: How to Restore the American Dream* (New York: New Press).

Websdale, N. (2001) *Policing the Poor: From Slave Plantation to Public Housing* (Boston: Northeastern University Press).

Western, B. (2007) 'Mass Imprisonment and Economic Inequality (III. Who We Punish: The Carceral State).' *Social Research, 74*, 509–532.

Which (2012) 'North East hardest hit by debt' [On-line]. Retrieved from: http://press.which.co.uk/whichpressreleases/north-east-hardest-hit-by-debt/ [accessed 5 March 2014].

Whitehead, M. and Doran, T. (2011) 'The North-South Health Divide.' *BMJ, 342*, d584–d584.

Whitehead, M. (Chair), Bambra, C., Barr, B. et al. (2014) *Due North: Report of the Inquiry on Health Equity for the North* (Liverpool and Manchester: University of Liverpool and Centre for Local Economic Strategies). Retrieved from: http://www.cles.org.uk/wp-content/uploads/2014/10/Due-North-Report-of-the-Inquiry-on-Health-Equity-in-the-North-final.pdf [accessed 20 November 2014].

Whyte, B. and Ajetunmobi, T. (2012) *Still 'The Sick Man of Europe'? Scottish Mortality in a European Context, 1950–2010* (Glasgow: Glasgow Centre for

Population Health). Retrieved from: http://www.gcph.co.uk/assets/0000/3606/Scottish_Mortality_in_a_European_Context_2012_v11_FINAL_bw.pdf [accessed 20 November 2014].

Wilkinson, R. and Pickett, K. (2010) *The Spirit Level: Why Equality Is Better for Everyone* (London: Penguin).

Wilkinson, R.G. and Pickett, K.E. (2008) 'Income Inequality and Socioeconomic Gradients in Mortality.' *American Journal of Public Health, 98*, 699–704.

Williams, P.L., Watt, C.G., Amero, M., et al. (2012) 'Affordability of a Nutritious Diet for Income Assistance Recipients in Nova Scotia (2002–2010).' *Canadian Journal of Public Health, 103*, 183–188.

Wills, J., Datta, K., Evans, Y., et al. (2010) *Global Cities at Work: New Migrant Divisions of Labour* (London: Pluto Press).

Winerip, M. and Schwirtz, M (2014) 'Rikers: Where Mental Illness Meets Brutality in Jail.' *New York Times*, July 14.

Wintour, P. (2013) 'Disabled Benefits Claimants Test: Atos Reports Found "Unacceptably Poor".' *Guardian*, July 22.

Wintour, P. and Inman, P. (2013) 'Nuclear Power Gets £10bn Financial Guarantee Boost.' *Guardian*, June 27.

Wisman, J.D. and Capehart, K.W. (2012) 'Creative Destruction, Economic Insecurity, Stress, and Epidemic Obesity.' In A. Offer, R. Pechey and S. Ulijaszek (eds.), *Insecurity, Inequality and Obesity in Affluent Societies* (Oxford: Oxford University Press for the British Academy).

Wolff, E.N. (2014) 'Household Wealth Trends in the United States, 1983–2010.' *Oxford Review of Economic Policy, 30*, 21–43.

Woolf, S. and Aron, L. (eds.) (2013) *US Health in International Perspective: Shorter Lives, Poorer Health* (Washington, DC: National Academies Press).

World Bank (2014) 'Life Expectancy at Birth, Male.' World Bank Indicators [On-line]. Retrieved from: http://data.worldbank.org/indicator/SP.DYN.LE00.MA.IN [accessed 20 November 2014].

World Health Organization (1978) 'Declaration of Alma-Ata, International Conference on Primary Health Care, Alma-Ata, USSR, 6–12 September.' World Health Organization [On-line]. Retrieved from: http://www1.umn.edu/humanrts/instree/alma-ata.html [accessed 6 October 2014].

Young, L.R. and Nestle, M. (2002) 'The Contribution of Expanding Portion Sizes to the US Obesity Epidemic.' *American Journal of Public Health, 92*, 246–249.

Young, L.R. and Nestle, M. (2007) 'Portion Sizes and Obesity: Responses of Fast-Food Companies.' *Journal of Public Health Policy, 28*, 238–248.

Index

Note: locators followed by n refer to notes.

Printed and bound by CPI Group (UK) Ltd, Croydon, CR0 4YY

.